Series Editor: Brian H Edwards

DayOne

Egypt
Land of Moses, monuments and mummies

Right: *Pyramids are one of the great defining images of Egypt*

Ancient Egyptian society

The concept of *Maat* was all-important for the ancient Egyptians. Balance, order and harmony were essential to a well-oiled society. Hard work was the lot of many and is revealed in the mortal remains of Egyptians. Ideally the next life would have fields that were blessed with no pests or failed harvests, and would be the perfect representation of *Maat*. In Predynastic and early Dynastic times (see Glossary on page 112), before the union of Upper and Lower Egypt, the rulers of Upper Egypt were called *nesu*, meaning 'he of the sedge', a grass-like herb, translated as 'King of Upper Egypt' or 'King of the South'. By contrast, the rulers of Lower Egypt used the title *bit*, meaning 'he of the bee', because of the proliferation of bees amongst the flowers, translated as 'King of Lower Egypt' or 'King of the North'. In later times, after the union of Upper and Lower Egypt, the rulers used the title *nesu-bit*, which meant 'he of the sedge and the bee', which is conventionally translated as 'King of Upper and Lower Egypt' or 'King of the South and North'.

Daily life was organised along a set pattern with Pharaonic Egypt being divided into forty-two administrative districts or nomes. They considered the ben-ben stone, (see the Box: Noah and the ben-ben stone on page 11) replicated the place where the first rays of the sun hit the earth and it was pyramid in shape. It formed the top of Pyramids and Obelisks (see Glossary on page 112). Society followed this pattern, [illegible] became an increasingly important symbol in the land.

The importance of *maat* can be seen in the order of society, the one responsible for maintaining or regaining *maat* was the king (pharaoh) and he was at the pinnacle of life on earth.

Above: *The King's authority revealed in the magnificent throne of Tutankhamun*

Noah and the ben-ben stone

As a sacred bird of the city of [illegible] (Heliopolis), the Egyptian benu-bird was the prototype for the Greek phoenix and was connected with the [illegible] and rebirth. In the [illegible] texts it appears as a yellow wagtail, [illegible] the Book of the Dead (see page 92). It is represented as a kind of grey heron. According to the Heliopolitan tradition, the world began as a watery chaos called Nun, from which the sun god Atum ("the All" or the "Complete One") emerged on a mound. Atum is said to have flown over the primeval waters as a bird, before coming to rest on a rock, or primeval mound (the ben-ben) that rose from the waters. The hieroglyphic script uses the image of a heron perched on a stick to write the word, "flood," and the benu-bird presides over the flood.

This myth could have been based on the episode of Noah recorded in Genesis 8 where he sent out two birds, the raven and the dove, to determine if the worldwide flood had receded. This was a rebirth for the world, as everything apart from the Ark and its inhabitants had been destroyed. As the Ark came to rest on the mountains of Ararat (in modern day Turkey), the first view that Noah and his family had of the dry earth (Genesis 8:13) may have been a mountain peak—hence the pyramid shape?

Egyptian bureaucracy was complex, and the centre of the maze was the institution of kingship, so it was vitally important to have not only a strong king but also powerful, wise and cunning advisors to maintain the stability of the country.

Egyptian Religion

The State religion was concerned with maintaining the divine order of *maat* to keep chaos at bay. Temples and priests served as a perpetual reminder that order was to be maintained for the good of the people. Religion dominated every aspect of life, and as the pinnacle of society, the king came to be regarded as the son of the god Ra on earth, (see page 118 for the chief gods of Egypt) and the chief prophets in the temples were among his most trusted advisors (Exodus 7:1–2).

Women, unusually for the ancient world, were on a legal equal footing with men, including for wages. Another demonstration of the equality of the sexes was that men and women both wore makeup and earrings. (Exodus 32:2–4). Plenty of moisturiser was applied to the face and most

King
Small group of trusted advisors
Coutriers who do the King's bidding
Governors of provinces
Mayors and skilled craftesman
Foreman and Overseers
Workers in the fields and in the cities
Unskilled peasants at the bottom

The order of Egyptian society

Facing page: *The Statue of Ramesses II in Karnak Temple proclaims his might and power*

Terror, temples and ancient texts

Thebes (modern Luxor) stood on both sides of the Nile and was the 'Thebes of the Greeks', celebrated for its hundred gates by Homer in his Iliad. In grandeur and extent it can only be compared to Nineveh and Babylon

Thebes was the ancient capital of Upper Egypt, mentioned in the Bible only in Jeremiah 46:25, Ezekiel 30:14–16, and Nahum 3:8. The Assyrians first captured Thebes in the time of Sargon II (Isaiah 20:1), then by Ashurbanipal (Ezra 4:10) before being delivered into the hand of the Babylonian Nebuchadnezzar II (Jeremiah 46:24–26).

Terror from the North

Ashurbanipal, the last great king of Assyria, succeeded to the throne when his father, Esarhaddon (2 Kings 19:37; Ezra 4:2), died on his way to campaign in Egypt in 669 BC. Esarhaddon's death caused the Pharaoh Taharqa, whom Sennacherib's spokesman had thirty-two years earlier called, 'that splintered reed of a staff which pierces a man's hand and wounds him if he leans on it' (Isaiah 36:6), to launch an offensive against the Assyrian garrison stationed at Memphis in 667 BC. Ashurbanipal despatched his rapid response units and retook the lost territory. In the Pergamum museum in Berlin is a large stone stela of Esarhaddon with the much smaller figures of Baalu king of Tyre and Pharaoh Taharqa cowering in fear before him. When Taharqa's nephew Tantamani became Pharaoh, he tried to regain control of Memphis and the Delta region. In response, Ashurbanipal reacted with another invasion, but this time he did not stop and pushed down the Nile to Thebes. The fall of Thebes in 664 BC is a key date for the history of the ancient world in general and the Old Testament in particular and is

Above: *Pylon Entrance to the Great Temple of Karnak*

CONTENTS

 First printed 2009

A CIP record is held at The British Library ISBN 978-1-84625-179-5

Published by Day One Publications Ryelands Road, Leominster, HR6 8NZ

01568 613 740 FAX 01568 611 473 email: sales@dayone.co.uk www.dayone.co.uk

Design: Kathryn Chedgzoy Printed by Polskabook, Poland

Dedication: For Luke

'The blessed land'

Egypt, the fabled land of romance, intrigue, mystery and terror, but above all of fabulous wealth and glittering gold. Since Napoleon's invasion in the 1790s, and the incredible discovery of Tutankhamun's intact tomb in the Valley of the Kings in 1922, the world has been increasingly drawn to books, films, museums and exhibitions that focus on the land of the Pharaohs.

In the centre of a garden nestles a rectangular pool containing lotus and other exotic water plants. The air is filled with heady and fragrant perfumes intoxicating the senses, emanating from jasmine, oleander, mimosa and dwarf chrysanthemums. Encircling them are pomegranate, date palm and sycamore fig trees, all producing a magnificent effect. The palace of a king or the dwelling of a noble would have included numerous luxuries including beautiful gardens, where the owners could be indulged, with servants waiting on their every need. However, the harsh truth was that in the royal court intrigue was ever-present and assassination a possibility; the battlefield was violent and all faced the reality of life under an unrelenting sun, where disease, danger, the displeasure of the gods, and an early death were all too common.

Here, the abundance of buildings, temples and royal mummies enable us to come face to face with the ancient Egyptians. But Egypt is not by any means a squeezed lemon. Who can tell how many more thrilling finds await the diligent archaeologist on site, or the historian in the museum or university? As these come to light, they will help to perpetuate interest in the 'blessed land', as it was known in ancient times; they will also fuel the knowledge of those who love and study the Bible, for Egypt played a major role in the story of the patriarchs and early Israel.

Through the pages of this Travel Guide, whether at home or in Egypt, we will explore this ancient world of beauty and mystery.

Facing page:
The River Nile has been enjoyed and used since earliest times

1 Red and Black lands

Egypt is the greatest oasis in the greatest desert in the world. In ancient times it stretched from the Mediterranean Sea in the north to the First Cataract at Aswan in the south, a distance of 1207 km (750 mi) by river

In Egypt, the River Nile glistens in the intense sunlight, whilst groves of dates, palms and tamarisk give protection to multitudes of bright flowers that bloom with rich and intense colour. The cliffs at the edge of the desert, seen to such good effect in the west at Luxor, glow and shine with deep and rich hues at sunrise and sunset. The night sky is ablaze with the glory of stars and planets.

The ancient Greeks were Egypt's first tourists and after 500 BC began to write about this strange land at a time when Egyptian civilization was drawing towards the close of its three thousand year existence. Alexander the Great, and his general Ptolemy, artificially preserved the culture in their own way. Under the Romans it faded rapidly and was stamped out completely by the Arab invaders of AD 639 to 646. The glories of Ancient Egypt were largely hidden from view for fourteen hundred years, from the fall of Rome to Napoleon's expedition of 1798. Then, in the early nineteenth century, explorers and the first diggers began to unearth the magnificence of the ancient past—the land of myth became the land of wonder.

Egypt is on the northeast shoulder of Africa, bordered by the Mediterranean Sea to the north, which the ancient Egyptians called the 'Great Green', deserts to the south and west and the Red Sea to the east. It consists geographically of two areas, the northern one, including the Delta closest to the Mediterranean Sea, called Lower Egypt, and the southern area called Upper Egypt (Isaiah 11:11).

Above: *Kemet, the black favoured land, and Deshret, the red feared land*

Facing page: *The Sphinx on the Giza plateau is one of the most famous landmarks in the whole world. The face of the sphinx is probably that of Djedefre a 4th Dynasty Pharaoh and son of Khufu*

The river of life

The Greek geographer Hecataeus famously wrote that 'Egypt is the gift of the Nile'. The Nile is like a strand of precious blue set against the tawny-coloured desert. Any vegetation that sprouted, and all livestock that grazed, were dependent on its waters for their existence. Almost one hundred years ago Rudyard Kipling wrote: 'Going up the Nile is like running the gauntlet before eternity. Till one has seen it, one does not realise the amazing thinness of that little damp trickle of life that steals along undefeated through the jaws of established death. A rifle shot would cover the widest limits of cultivation; a bowshot would reach the narrower. The weight of the desert is on one, every day and every hour.'

That 'little damp trickle' is 6,670km (4,160mi) in length, making the River Nile the longest river in the world. The Nile has two main tributaries: the White Nile and the Blue Nile. The White Nile rises in the great lakes of Africa, and flows from southern Rwanda through Tanzania, Lake Victoria, Uganda and Southern Sudan. The Blue Nile starts at Lake Tana in Ethiopia flowing into Sudan from the southeast and the two parts join near Khartoum the capital of Sudan. This means that less than a quarter of the Nile flows through Egypt, creating the fertile green valley from 1.6km (1mi) to 32km (20mi) in width through the desert. However the flow of water in ancient times was not always consistent and nilometers were set up to gauge the flow so as to help in ascertaining the prospects for a rich or poor harvest. This rise and fall is reflected in Amos 8:8.

The annual inundation usually occurred between the months of July and October, then the planting of crops could take place in the deep rich black mud and silt between November and February, yielding a harvest between March and June, when hopefully the whole process would begin again. If the river flow was not as expected it could result in flood or famine; either way, disaster would loom, especially if provision had not been made for this eventuality (Genesis 41:29–30). Water from the Nile was directed to the fields

***Right:** The River Nile has been the life blood of the country since ancient times*

through channels of decreasing size, and the smallest could be opened or closed by moving mud with the foot. This explains the seemingly curious statement in Deuteronomy 11:10 about foot irrigation.

By the time of Ptolemy I, 305 to 285 BC, Egypt supported a population estimated to be seven million people. The land was rich and fertile, and difficult to attack when Egypt was at the height of her power; it would eventually provide Rome with a third of its corn.

The desert of death

In contrast to the lush river valley, the western desert had an evil reputation with hot dry winds blowing across the sand, which dealt with the unwary in dramatic fashion; more then one army was swallowed up, disappearing completely: Cambyses, the Persian king lost his army as it marched to Siwa c 520 BC. However, the Delta—a triangle of low-lying green land about 150 miles in each direction from the river—and the coastal regions of Egypt, have high temperatures and humidity in the summer with heavy rains in the winter. A hot scorching wind called the *Khamsin* blows across the Delta between March and May, which in the days before air conditioning would leave people fatigued and irritable. Egypt's variable climate encouraged many diseases to flourish (Deuteronomy 7:15), and Moses warned the Israelites that if they were not faithful to God, he would afflict them with these diseases (Deuteronomy 28:60). Today, however, the climate of Egypt is beneficial to many, and the warm Mediterranean breezes give the country a year-round growing season making it a suitable place for the tourist.

Ancient names to describe Egypt

The ancient Egyptians gave various names to the Land:

Tawy = the two lands, upper and lower Egypt.

Ta Mery = the beloved land. The ancient people were not obsessed with death but desired the next life to be a perfect replica of this one, so the survival of the body was imperative for the soul to exist in the next life.

Kemet = the black land. The black land after the inundation of the Nile when the black deposit was sown with seed and a harvest could then be guaranteed.

Deshret = the red land, the endless desert to the east and west. This is where the goddess Sekhmet dwelt, the place of fear and fire.

The dryness of arid wastelands along the Nile Valley naturally dried out human and animal remains, and mummification developed naturally. The desolate regions surrounding Egypt established natural borders that were fairly easy to defend, and perilous to enter. Except in the Delta, where, if any walked away to the east or west from the river until they needed water, they would have died of thirst before they could walk back again for a drink, a fact not lost on the Hebrews (Exodus 17:3).

Right: Pyramids are one of the great defining images of Egypt

Ancient Egyptian society

The concept of *Maat* was all-important for the ancient Egyptians. Balance, order and harmony were essential to a well-oiled society. Hard work was the lot of many and is revealed in the mortal remains of Egyptians. Ideally the next life would have fields that were blessed with no pests or failed harvests, and would be the perfect representation of *Maat*. In Predynastic and early Dynastic times (see Glossary on page 112) , before the union of Upper and Lower Egypt, the rulers of Upper Egypt were called *nesw*, meaning 'he of the sedge', a grass-like herb, translated as 'King of Upper Egypt' or 'King of the South'. By contrast, the rulers of Lower Egypt used the title *bit*, meaning 'he of the bee', because of the proliferation of bees amongst the flowers, translated as 'King of Lower Egypt' or 'King of the North'. In later times, after the union of Upper and Lower Egypt, the rulers used the title *nesw-bit*, which meant 'he of the sedge and the bee', which is conventionally translated as 'King of Upper and Lower Egypt' or 'King of the South and North'.

Daily life was organised along a set pattern with Pharaonic Egypt being divided into forty-two administrative districts or nomes. They considered the ben-ben stone, (see the Box: Noah and the ben-ben stone on page 11) replicated the place where the first rays of the sun hit the earth and it was pyramid in shape. It formed the top of Pyramids and Obelisks (see Glossary on page 112). Society followed this pattern, as it became an increasingly important symbol in the land.

The importance of *maat* can be seen in the order of society, the one responsible for maintaining or regaining *maat* was the king (pharaoh) and he was at the pinnacle of life on earth.

Above: The King's authority revealed in the magnificent throne of Tutankhamun

Noah and the ben-ben stone

As a sacred bird of the city of On (Heliopolis), the Egyptian benu-bird was the prototype for the Greek phoenix and was connected with the sun and rebirth. In the pyramid texts it appears as a yellow wagtail, but in the Book of the Dead (see page 92) it is represented as a kind of grey heron. According to the Heliopolitan Tradition, the world began as a watery chaos called Nun, from which the sun god Atum ('the All' or the 'Complete One') emerged on a mound. Atum is said to have flown over the primeval waters as a bird, before coming to rest on a rock, or primeval mound (the ben-ben) that rose from the waters. The hieroglyphic script uses the image of a heron perched on a stick to write the word, 'flood,' and the benu-bird presides over the flood.

This myth could have been based on the episode of Noah recorded in Genesis 8 where he sent out two birds, the raven and the dove, to determine if the worldwide flood had receded. This was a rebirth for the world, as everything apart from the Ark and its inhabitants had been destroyed. As the Ark came to rest on the mountains of Ararat (in modern day Turkey), the first view that Noah and his family had of the dry earth (Genesis 8:13) may have been a mountain peak—hence the pyramid shape?

Egyptian bureaucracy was complex, and the centre of the maze was the institution of kingship, so it was vitally important to have not only a strong king but also powerful, wise and cunning advisors to maintain the stability of the country.

Egyptian Religion

The State religion was concerned with maintaining the divine order of *maat* to keep chaos at bay. Temples and priests served as a perpetual reminder that order was to be maintained for the good of the people. Religion dominated every aspect of life, and as the pinnacle of society, the king came to be regarded as the son of the god Ra on earth, (see page 118 for the chief gods of Egypt) and the chief prophets in the temples were among his most trusted advisors (Exodus 7:1–2).

Women, unusually for the ancient world, were on a legal equal footing with men, including wage earning. Another demonstration of the equality of the sexes was that men and women both wore makeup and earrings, (Exodus 32:2–4). Plenty of moisturiser was applied to the face and most people shaved

The order of Egyptian society

off all body hair to combat the problem of head lice, ticks and other afflictions. When Pharaoh (from *per-aa* Great House) commanded that Joseph was to be released from prison, to make himself acceptable at court Joseph shaved and changed his clothes (Genesis 41:14). The cost of clothes was prohibitive for most, so the majority of people owned only an over garment with a couple of changes of loincloth.

People drank water from wells or straight from the Nile (Exodus 7:24), though river water had to be drawn with care as, not only fish, but also hippopotamus, crocodile, and water snakes inhabited the Nile. At times the water was not only unpalatable but also dangerous as it contained many harmful organisms (unknown to the Egyptians) and residues. The young king Tutankhamun preferred white wine, but most people drank beer, which meant they went through life in a slightly intoxicated state. It was brewed from barley and bread and had the consistency of vegetable soup so it had to be strained or drunk through a straw. Cough drops, mouthwash and chewing gum were also invented in Egypt.

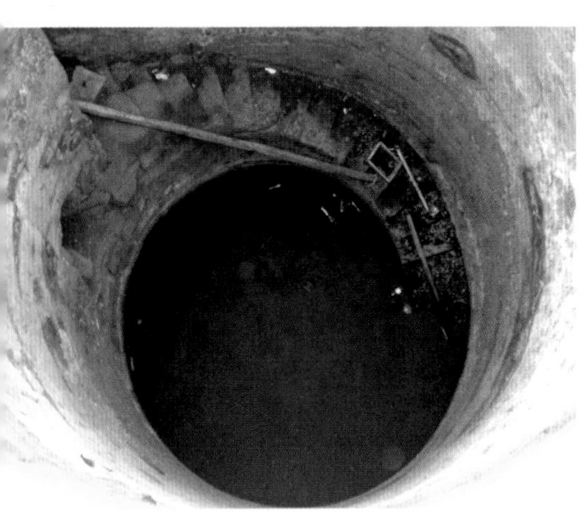

***Above:** Nilometers used to measure the flood levels of the river each year*

Food and drink

Basic food came from or near the Nile, and meat could include goat, mutton or pork (though the latter not for the priests). The poorer end of society existed on bread, onions and other salad, whereas those with a better lifestyle could enjoy wildfowl, ducks and geese, with a favourite dish of the upper classes being crispy duck roasted in honey.

The importance of Language

Arabic is the language used in Egypt today, although the picture language of the ancient Egyptians, known as hieroglyphics, is synonymous with its history. Ancient Egyptian is one of the oldest recorded languages (probably only Sumerian is older) and it has a documented history longer by far than any other. The work of the scribe was highly respected:

'By day write with your fingers, recite by night. Befriend

Left: Palestine Railways train ticket from Haifa to Suez used by Corporal Harry Lambert on 11 January 1943

the scroll and the palette—it is more fulfilling than wine!' Papyrus Lansing, from the New Kingdom.

Hieroglyphics.
Hieroglyphs are written in horizontal lines from right to left or left to right, downwards in columns, or curved around objects. Sometimes two sets of hieroglyphs will face each other. The direction in which to read an inscription often starts with a person, animal or bird, and the inscription would be read from the front of them.

Hieratic. This was used by the priests as an adaptation of the hieroglyphic script through most of its history, often used for administrative purposes and personal letters. For speed it was usually written in black ink (occasionally red to mark out a significant section), applied by means of a brush made out of a rush stem.

Demotic. This is the writing that the ordinary people used and the word means 'of the people'. It can be traced from the Late Period down to late Roman times (c. 664BC to fifth century AD). Demotic is derived from the ancient Greek *demotika*, meaning popular. The demotic record was used mainly for legal, administrative, and commercial purposes, although from the Ptolemaic period it was employed for literary, scientific and religious texts.

Coptic. This is the final stage of the language, after the old scripts went into decline during Egypt's Roman and Christian periods. Coptic is derived from the Arabic *gubti* which is a corruption of the Greek *Aiguptious*, and simply means Egyptian. The Arabs used this term after the conquest of Egypt in the seventh century to denote the native inhabitants of the country, and it is still in use by the Copts.

Above: Tourists on a Nile cruise boat

Above: *The train journey through the Red and Black land*

Left: *Hieroglyphics at Philae Temple*

Bottom: *Hieroglyphic writing from Luxor temple spelling out the name of Ramesses II*

Through Egypt with the Bible

Egypt is mentioned throughout the Bible, from Genesis 12:10 to Revelation 11:8. According to Genesis 10:6 and 13, Mizraim the grandson of Noah and son of Ham is the ancestor of the Egyptians, and Mizraim is the name for Egypt in the Bible. In Arabic, Egypt is *Misr* after Mizraim, although Psalm 105:23 also calls it 'the land of Ham'. Some writers have suggested that the founder of

***Above:** Aerial photo of a farmhouse on the west bank of the Nile at Luxor. The style of house has changed little over the millennia*

***Above:** Camels used for long-distance travel (Genesis 12:16 and Exodus 9:3). This one is in the Sinai peninsular*

Egypt's first dynasty, Menes, was the same as Mizraim.

Egypt had a profound influence on God's people, the Israelites, and is referred to geographically, symbolically and spiritually, as the place both of refuge and oppression. This duality is first seen in the book of Genesis when Abram (later Abraham) was struggling to survive in a time of famine, and he made the long journey into Egypt to escape the severest part of the famine. He visited the country as a place of refuge but it became a place of captivity and oppression, for whilst there, Abram feared for his life and reasoned that the King (probably Khety II) was going to take his wife Sarai (later Sarah) for himself. When it was discovered that she was not Abram's sister but his wife, they were allowed to leave unharmed, (Genesis 12:10–20).

Joseph, famous for his so called 'coat of many colours', and the great-grandson of Abraham, was sold into slavery by his jealous brothers for twenty shekels, the price of a slave in the Middle Kingdom. The traders brought him to Egypt and he was sold on to Potiphar the captain of the royal guard. Nevertheless, Joseph did extremely well in handling Potiphar's business matters, but Potiphar's wife endeavoured to take advantage of Joseph who refused to cooperate with her wishes; as a consequence he was unfairly thrown into jail. After many years he correctly interpreted the dream of the king (probably Sesostris III) and was released and was eventually promoted to the second most important figure in the land, able to influence for good both state and family life (Genesis 37:12 to 47:12).

In the time of Joseph, Egypt was the great superpower in the region and, in the course of time, the Israelites settled in the Delta and were eventually enslaved. From here, under the leadership of Moses, they set out on the great Exodus from the land, (Exodus 12). As the ancient Egyptians followed a ten-day week, could the ten plagues have been directed at all areas and times of life? The Israelites, being in the land for 430 years would have become accustomed to this, so the seven-day principle had to be reinstated at Sinai (Exodus 20:8–11). The Exodus of the Hebrew people is undoubtedly the most famous event connected with Egypt, although they often yearned to return (Numbers 11:4 to 6). In later centuries alliances were made with the military might of Egypt's army in preference to relying on the strength and salvation promised by the Lord their God (for example see Isaiah 31:1).

The Bible deliberately draws attention to the special love Solomon had for the daughter of Pharaoh (1 Kings 3:1, 7:8, 9:16 and 24); she may have been the lady referred to in the Song of Solomon, (Song of Songs 1:4–7). An 'Egyptian papyrus column capital' in the Garden Tomb, Jerusalem, may have come from the Egyptian building that lies under the nave of the nearby basilica of St Etienne—could it have been the tomb of Solomon's Egyptian Queen (2 Chronicles 8:11)?

In the reign of Rome's greatest emperor Caesar Augustus, Jesus of Nazareth, along with his family, found refuge in Egypt (Matthew 2:13–18); perhaps the gifts of the Magi (Matthew 2:11) financed their journey, since gold was, and still is, an international currency, and incense was valuable for use in the temples and homes alike, and myrrh was used both in medicine and the process of embalming. The fact that God

Top: *The gold mummy mask of the General and High Priest Wendjebauendjed reveals the extraordinary care the ancient Egyptians took to preserve the dead*

Above: *Egyptian papyrus column capital in the Garden Tomb, Jerusalem, which may have come from the tomb of Solomon's Egyptian Queen*

Above: *Carvings of the different crowns of Egypt flanked by images defaced by early Christians to fulfil the requirements of the second commandment, Deuteronomy 5:8. From the temple at Dendera*

had chosen Egypt as a safe place for his infant Son was a great source of pride to Egyptian Christians. According to legend, the holy family travelled as far south as Deir el-Maharraq, near Asyut. If they did, they would no doubt have travelled in sailing boats on the Nile.

Christianity in Egypt

The history of Christianity in Egypt can be traced a long way back. Tradition claims the apostle Mark brought Christianity to Egypt in the early part of the first century AD. Eusebius, Bishop of Caesarea, in his *Ecclesiastic History*, states that Mark first came to Egypt between the first and third year of the reign of Emperor Claudius (Acts 18), which would be sometime between AD 41 and 44, and that he returned twenty years later to preach and evangelize (Mark 16:15). It is said that Mark's first convert in Alexandria was Anianus, a shoemaker who was later consecrated a bishop and became Patriarch of Alexandria after Mark's death. This succession of Patriarchs has remained unbroken down to the present day, making the Egyptian Christian, or Coptic, Church one of the oldest Christian churches in existence. Boutros-Boutros Ghali the former UN Secretary-General is an internationally renowned Copt.

Egyptology

After Napoleon's scholars explored Egypt, Giovanni Belzoni and other entrepreneurs started to ship artefacts back to Europe and an explosion of interest was

Above: *At Edfu market many items are displayed to attract the tourist and encourage them to take home a little bit of Egypt*

kindled. The science of studying Egypt academically began in 1822 with the deciphering of the hieroglyphic script by Jean-François Champollion. He was developing the work of the Englishman Thomas Young, the inventor of the wave theory of light and the first modern scholar to translate the Demotic script, who had shown how the Greek royal name Ptolemaios was spelt out in Egyptian hieroglyphics on the Rosetta Stone (see the next chapter). Then William Flinders Petrie and Howard Carter (discoverer of Tutankhamun's tomb) were instrumental in stirring the public's imagination followed by Hollywood's enthusiasm to depict Egypt as a land of wealth and mystery. Today, the many television programmes that highlight recent discoveries have resulted in the current general interest in Egyptology.

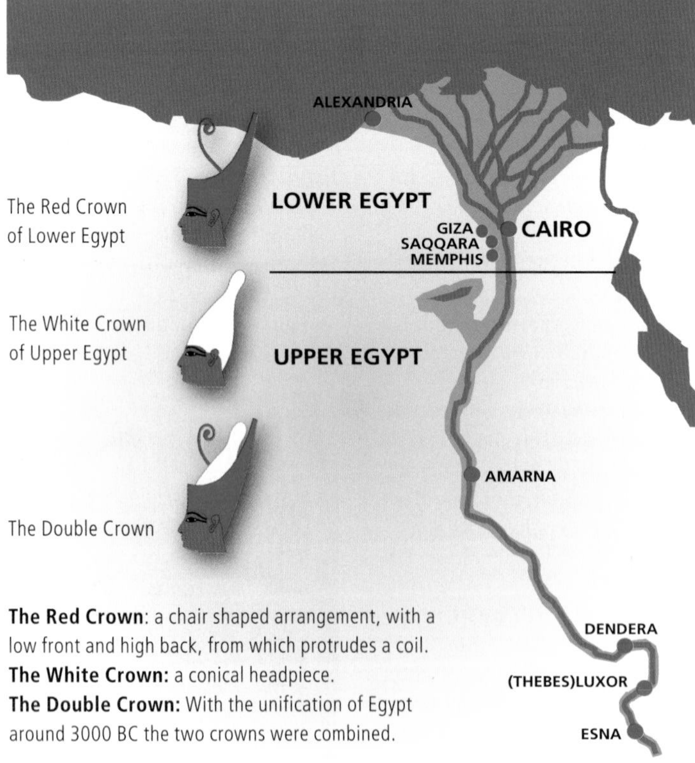

The Red Crown: a chair shaped arrangement, with a low front and high back, from which protrudes a coil.
The White Crown: a conical headpiece.
The Double Crown: With the unification of Egypt around 3000 BC the two crowns were combined.

See the picture (page 17) for more Egyptian crowns

TRAVEL INFORMATION

Travel to and around Egypt is relatively easy, especially if you join a prearranged tour that will take the stress out of sightseeing. For example see www.dayone.co.uk Those who travel on their own, or in a small party, should plan well ahead. Take advice, as there are areas it is not wise for tourists to travel into, and regulations change regarding visa requirements and exit fees. Also, obtain adequate insurance cover for any medical or other needs.

Websites

Please note that many sites and museums in Egypt do not have websites at present. Egyptian Tourist Authority www.egypt.travel/sitemap.php

Bird Watching

Egypt's strategic geographical position encourages migrant birds to pass through on their journeys between the breeding grounds of Europe and Asia and the wintering grounds of sub-Saharan Africa. For enthusiasts, the well-known 'bottleneck' at Suez is of international importance for birds of prey (Job 39:26) and storks (Leviticus 11:19), which concentrate in large numbers on spring and autumn migration. Even if you are not an ornithologist, a pair of binoculars will enhance the delights of any trip to Egypt.

Above: *Egypt's Red Sea coast boasts many fine resorts including that of Sharm El-Sheikh*

Scuba diving

Many Red Sea resorts are being developed to cater for the increasing numbers of tourists, and if it is possible to extend the visit after sightseeing, then a few days relaxing along the Red Sea is the best possible preparation before returning to the daily grind.

Above: *Bird's are everywhere. This sparrow is in a crevice at Edfu Temple*

Eating out

In Cairo there are a variety of places to eat and most hotels will allow non residents into their restaurants. Elsewhere in Egypt there are a great many food stalls and a few coffee shops where the seasoned traveller would be happy to eat. If you are in doubt it is best to go to a hotel.

2 Alexander's nose

The invasion of Egypt by Napoleon in 1798 contained double the number of ships that came against England in the Spanish Armada. Crucially though, Napoleon brought 167 scholars in his fleet who were to open the eyes of the world to Egypt's wonders

Among those scholars (known as savants from the French for 'knowing') were artists, inventors, mathematicians, scientists and writers comprising the intellectual cream of France. These people gave birth to Egyptology and produced many stunning works included in the *Description de l'Egypt* (Description of Egypt), which gave the first panoramic view of a world virtually unknown until then.

The Rosetta stone

The Rosetta Stone, discovered by a French officer in 1799 at Rosetta in the western Delta of Egypt, was surrendered to the British at the end of the Napoleonic war; it was taken to the British Museum in London in 1802. The stone is carved on black basalt and at the top is hieroglyphic writing, the second section is demotic Egyptian; the third is in Greek capital letters (known as 'uncial'). The Greek was translated relatively easily and proved to be part of a citation by Egyptian priests in Memphis to celebrate the first anniversary of the coronation of Ptolemy V in 196 BC. Recognising that the two Egyptian scripts were the equivalent text to the Greek was a major breakthrough and, once deciphered in 1822, enabled Jean-François Champollion and others to understand ancient Egyptian writing. The hieroglyphic script would have been known to Israel during their time in Egypt, and to Moses who was educated in the royal court of Pharaoh (Acts 7:22). Important proclamations in the ancient world were often recorded in three languages—the most famous of all being the sign above Jesus on the cross 'written in Aramaic, Latin and Greek' (John19:20).

Alexandria

Alexandria is a long thin city. This was the ancient metropolis of Lower Egypt, named after Alexander the Great who founded it in c.334 BC. It was the residence of the kings of Egypt for over 200 years. It is not mentioned in the Old Testament, but in the New Testament at the time of Stephen's

Facing page: *The Rosetta Stone, now housed in the British Museum in London, provided the key to the translation of the ancient Egyptian scripts*

Above: Roman Theatre at Alexandria on Egypt's Northern Coast

martyrdom, many Jews from Alexandria were in Jerusalem, where they had a synagogue (Acts 6:9); Apollos, was a native of this city (Acts 18:24), and possibly as many as 100,000 Jews resided in the city. Alexandria also possessed a famous library of 700,000 volumes, which was burned by the Saracens in AD 642. Here, in the middle of the third century BC, the Hebrew Bible was translated into Greek, and became known as the Septuagint version, indicated by the Roman numerals LXX for 70, from the tradition that seventy scholars were engaged in the translation.

Alexandria was a city famed for invention and innovation. In the third century BC the engineer Ctesibus, invented the pipe organ called the *hydralis*, where water pressure generated wind supply to pipes; although it had a tendency to gurgle, it was played in the arenas of the Roman Empire! Another engineer, Hero, is credited with inventing and putting into operation the first steam engine in Alexandria.

Recent underwater exploration has discovered over 300 huge blocks, some 75 tonnes in weight, that may represent the remains of the Pharos lighthouse—one of the seven wonders of the ancient world. On 10 August 30 BC Queen Cleopatra VII, the lover of Julius Caesar and Marc Anthony, died in this city probably from self-administered poison.

Alexander's nose

In September 31 BC, Caesar Augustus (then Octavian) defeated the coalition of Marc Anthony and Cleopatra at the sea battle of Actium before visiting the tomb of Alexander the Great. Augustus was descended from Alexander through his mother. His guides offered to take him to see tombs of the Ptolemaic dynasty, but Augustus answered, 'I have come to see a King and not dead people.'

Alexander had died in Babylon in 323 BC possibly poisoned by Ptolemy I. His embalmed body was transported in sumptuous splendour in a gold and crystal coffin first to Memphis and then here where it became the city's most sacred relic. Alexander's tomb stood at the crossroads of the city's two main avenues, a site now lost but probably located where the Mosque of the prophet Daniel stands today.

To enable Augustus to pay his respects, Alexander's mummy was temporarily removed and displayed in public; Augustus crowned the mummy's head with a golden diadem and placed flowers on the body. Dio Cassius, the second century Roman historian, records that as Augustus bent over to kiss the great conqueror, he accidentally broke off Alexander's nose!

The church school at Alexandria

Perhaps the greatest contribution of Egypt to early Christianity was the Catechetical School of Alexandria, called the *Didascalia* (from the Greek word for teacher). It is claimed to be the oldest school of Christian religion in the world, founded around AD 190 by the scholar Pantaenus. Many bishops and leaders of the early Christian Church, both in Egypt and abroad, were educated at the *Didascalia* under such great theologians as Clement and Origen (called the 'Father of Theology'). Jerome, who translated the Bible into Latin (the Vulgate version) in the fifth century AD, visited the school both to debate and exchange ideas.

Athanasius, born in Alexandria around AD 299 was the most important Church Father connected with the city, he championed traditional teaching against Arius, who denied the deity of Christ. Athanasius was deeply affected by the terrible persecutions and sufferings of Christians under the Emperor Diocletian and Licinius. Eusebius, the historian and advisor to the Roman emperor Constantine, records that entire towns were massacred for confessing Christ.

Left: *Roman Pompey Pillar at Alexandria*

Athanasius and Arius

Athanasius was involved in the profound debates between Bishop Alexander and Arius (Arianism), regarding the eternal existence of Jesus Christ. Arius claimed that Jesus had not always existed, but had been created by God the Father, and taught that 'there was, when he was not' which, according to the Bible, is totally unacceptable (Colossians 1:15–16). Tertullian, another early church leader, had superbly summed up the Bible's teaching about God by stating, 'They are three unique persons with one shared substance.'

To work through these mighty issues, Constantine, the first Roman emperor to embrace Christianity, held a council at Nicaea in Turkey, when many of the finest minds in the Church came together to debate this subject. Out of their deliberations came the Nicene Creed, which was so strenuously promoted by Athanasius that an expression came into being, *Athanasius contra mundam*, Athanasius against the world.

***Above:** Athanasius the early church father who helped to compile the Nicene Creed*

Part of the Nicene Creed reads: 'I believe in one God, the Father Almighty, Maker of heaven and earth, and of all things visible and invisible. And in one Lord Jesus Christ, the only-begotten Son of God, begotten of the Father before all worlds; God of God, Light of Light, very God of very God; begotten, not made, being of one substance with the Father, by whom all things were made…'

Goshen

The Israelites settled in Goshen, a region close to the border of Israel, possibly with the intention of returning home when the famine had ceased (Genesis 45:10–11). However, life in Egypt was very agreeable, especially when Joseph was in a prominent position to help his family and people (Genesis 47:11–12). Following Joseph's death, the majority of Israelites remained in this area until the Exodus (Exodus 8:22). Sometime later, Egypt was invaded by the Hyksos (shepherd kings) and life changed dramatically for the Hebrews. The Hyksos occupied Lower Egypt for over one hundred years before the liberation started under Pharaoh Seqenenre Tao II (See page 54).

As Goshen is located in the Delta region, it is not easy to trace the Israelites since little has survived due to agricultural activity and a high water table, resulting in the many mud brick structures vanishing.

Left: The Israelites had to make bricks in Goshen. Those in the foreground at a modern village are very similar in size to the ancient ones familiar to the Hebrew slaves

Pithom and Ramesses

These storage cities were the centre of Israelite oppression (Exodus 1:11). Tel El-Maskhuta was believed to be the site of Pithom. Storerooms found near the Temple may be part of the stores mentioned in Exodus. Others consider they date from the time of Ramesses II (the late date Pharaoh for the Exodus), or they may be the remains of a fort. However, the latest theory is that it is Tell er-Retaba that may be biblical Pithom, although limited excavation has so far not yielded any positive results.

Tell ed-Daba is believed to be the site of the city of Ramesses, and it was originally named Avaris by the Hyksos. Supporters of a late date for the Exodus consider it impossible that the Hebrews could have built a city prior to 1300 BC before a king with the name Ramesses lived. However, Genesis 47:11 shows that a place known as Ramesses, when Joseph was in Egypt, was functioning, and if the author of Exodus was writing retrospectively, might it originally have been named something else? A modern example is St Petersburg in Russia: first renamed Petrograd then Leningrad before finally reverting back to St Petersburg.

Tanis (Zoan of the Bible)

Zoan was constructed seven years after Hebron in Israel (Numbers 13:22). According to Psalm 78:12 and 43, the plagues of Egypt were revealed to the Israelites around here. This city was popularised by the Indiana Jones film *Raiders of the Lost Ark*, as the location of the Ark of the Covenant.

Where's the proof?

The Exodus of the Israelites from Egypt is one of the most contentious events in history. Archaeologists and historians have looked for signs to authenticate the biblical account and, as nothing has been positively identified, many remain sceptical as to its authenticity. However, Prof. K. A. Kitchen has wisely written, 'absence of evidence is not evidence of absence.' In the ancient world, no official record exists of anything detrimental to rulers or the land,

Moses and Maat

After exile in Midian (Exodus 2:15) Moses, at the age of eighty, was challenged by God to return to Egypt. The martyr Stephen claimed: 'Moses was educated in all the wisdom of the Egyptians and was powerful in speech and action' (Acts 7:22)—something Moses denied when trying to avoid being sent back into Egypt (Exodus 4:10). His education would have been comprehensive and extensive and much of his learning and ideas from Egypt would have stayed with him throughout his life. Maat was the principle that held ancient Egyptian society together and underpinned religious belief. Maat meant: balance, harmony, justice, order and truth, and was thought of as being a return to the moment of creation when all was perfect new and unsullied. Maat was represented by the goddess Maat, with an ostrich feather on her head, and she was present in the judgement at the weighing of the heart.

The phenomenon of the burning bush went against the natural order and balance of things (Exodus 3:3). On returning to Egypt Moses was instrumental, through the plagues, in upsetting the balance, harmony, and order of Egyptian life until the Israelites were granted permission to leave the country (Exodus 12:30).

for to record something was to perpetuate it. On the other hand, in Leiden Museum in the Netherlands, there is a papyrus written by Ipuwer that dates to the later 13th century BC, and some Egyptologists believe that the papyrus was a copy of an earlier Middle kingdom document. Ipuwer describes Egypt as afflicted by natural disasters and in a state of chaos, a topsy-turvy world where the poor have become rich, and the rich poor, and warfare, famine and death are everywhere. One symptom of this collapse of order is the lament that servants are leaving their servitude and acting rebelliously. Because of this, and statements like 'the River is blood', some have interpreted the document as a veiled Egyptian account of the Plagues and Exodus.

Left: *The donkey has been utilised in Egypt since time immemorial*

Right: Egypt had an efficient army through many years of its existence. These soldiers are painted on the wall of Deir El-Bahri

Sharq

Sharq (Qantara East) is a recent exciting discovery in North Sinai. The city was a strategic trading post, and in the Graeco–Roman period it became one of Egypt's busiest ports, second only to Alexandria. Its chequered history is a reminder of several military clashes, from the times of the Pharaohs to the early 1970s.

As the vital commercial and military stopover between Egypt and Asia, it became the starting point of the famous Horus military road, known in the Bible as 'the road through Philistine country' (Exodus 13:17), which operated from ancient Egyptian times until the Ottoman period.

The route of the Exodus

Although the Bible records the route taken by the fleeing Hebrews (Exodus 12:37; 13:17–20; 14:2 and Numbers 33), there is as yet no archaeological evidence of the forty-year wandering of the children of Israel in the Sinai Peninsula. The Sea of Reeds is a traditional route of the Exodus, an area north of the Gulf of Suez, but a shallow area of water could hardly drown the Egyptian army! Some have speculated that the crossing may have occurred at Nuweiba on the Red Sea. It appears King Solomon built his navy near here (1 Kings 9:26). If this was the crossing point, the Israelites would have come to Mount Sinai, in Midian, in what is now Saudi Arabia (Galatians 4:25). The Sinai peninsular is the

Left: The Bible states that the Israelites crossed the Red Sea to escape Pharaoh's army

The Hand of God

The hand is mentioned a surprising number of times in relation to the events of the Exodus (Exodus 3:19, 20; 4:2,4,6,7,17,20; 6:1; 7:4,5,15,17,19; 8:5,6,17; 9:3,15, 22; 10:12,21,22; 12:11; 13:3,9,14,16, 14,16,21,26,27; 15:6,9,12). Some seem to be superfluous, but when read against the belief system of ancient Egypt, the holy power of the one true God shines through in contrast to the creative vigour of the Egyptian false deity, Atum.

The ancient Egyptians believed that before creation there had been a state of non-existence that was characterised by total darkness and limitless waters (cf. Genesis 1:2). From this emerged a creator who established the universe. The Pyramid texts contain a reference to creation, which is mentioned in utterance 527. Atum, the creator god, was alone on the primeval hill (see the Box: Noah and the ben-ben stone on page 11) and had no consort to share in the creative act, so with his hand he performs an act of self-fornication to bring about creation.

This belief about the creation of everything goes against the teaching of the Bible which clearly reveals it is by the word of God that all came into being (Genesis 1:3 and John1:1 to 2). It may be of interest to note that it was sometimes claimed that Atum was originally a serpent, a form to which he was said to be destined to return when the world ends, only changing into a human during its existence (Genesis 3:1, and Isaiah 14:16).

traditional location of the forty years wanderings. In antiquity, acacia trees occurred in large numbers here and were used in the production of charcoal. Acacia (Hebrew *Shittim* as AV) trees survive for many years because of their long roots, which locate moisture deep below the surface. The Israelites had access to trees like this, which were used in the construction of the Tabernacle (eg Exodus 25:13).

Mount Sinai/Horeb

The location of Mount Sinai/Horeb has caused considerable debate; two of the favoured sites are Ras es-safsafeh and Jebel Musa. The second is favoured by many, and the monastery of St Catherine is located here. At Sinai, Moses sat by the well (Exodus 2:15), the burning bush was not consumed (Exodus 3:1, Acts 7:29–30), the Law was given (Exodus 19:2), and Elijah ran

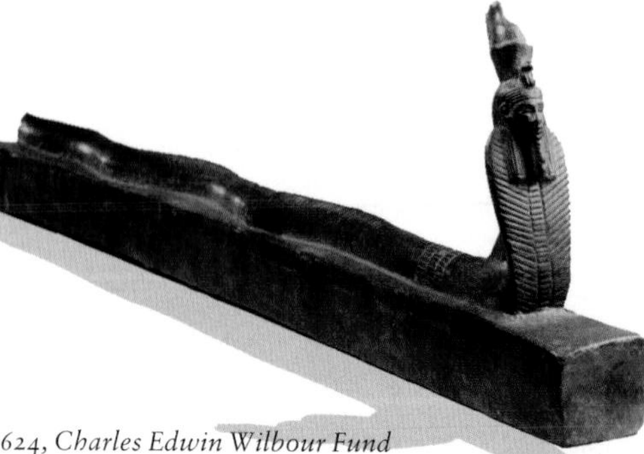

***Right:** The Egyptian god Atum as a human-headed Cobra. Bronze. Late Ptolemaic period, c. 664-30 BC. Provenance not known.*

Top Right: The Children of Israel travelled through the wilderness of Sinai

Right: The location of Mount Sinai is debated, but many favour this mountain of Jebel Musa. Visitors can ascend before dawn to view the sunrise

Below: Sign to Moses Mountain at Mount Sinai

here to escape the revenge of Queen Jezebel (1 Kings 19:8–13).

Suez Canal and El-Alamein

This remarkable engineering enterprise was begun on 25 April 1859 and the work was completed in March 1869—at the cost of the death of about 200 workers each year. The great advantage to shipping made it a target for the Nazis during the World War II, but Montgomery's defeat of Rommel stopped them acquiring it. The coastal town of El-Alamein is famous for being the location of one of the key battles of World War II. The Germans under Field Marshal Erwin Rommel swept across North Africa and threatened Alexandria and the Suez Canal; they were halted here in a last ditch defence by the British under the command of General Bernard Montgomery. Each October a commemorative service is held, but each year the number of veterans attending diminishes. Winston Churchill wrote of the Battle of El-Alamein: 'Before Alamein we never had a victory. After Alamein we never had a defeat.' About 11,000 soldiers lie in the war cemeteries.

Siwa Oasis

Siwa is attractive to visit, but to get to it some of the harshest terrain has to be navigated. Located here is the Temple of

Right: *The Mubarak peace bridge spanning the Suez Canal*

Nectanebo II, rock tombs of the 26th to 30th dynasty's and the Temple of Amasis, the presumed site of the oracle consulted by Alexander the Great. He travelled here in 331 BC—the first King of Egypt to undertake this journey—and was received as 'son of Zeus-Amun, master of all lands, unconquered until he is united with the gods', then crowned with the ram's horn crown (see Daniel 8:5–8). The Egyptians looked upon him as a divine being and saviour. Alexander the Great had asked to be buried at Siwa. In 1942 just before the battle of El-Alamein, the German Field Marshal Rommel made his own way to Siwa to see if he could outflank the British forces.

Bahariya Oasis

In 1996 about 3km (2mi) south of a temple of Alexander the Great, a donkey slipped and its foot was caught in a hole; excavations revealed numerous Egyptian mummies covered in gilt. To date, 100 mummies have been unearthed from the Valley of the Golden Mummies, but it is thought over 10,000 more are awaiting discovery, in what is said to be the largest single necropolis in Egypt.

What made so many Greek, Roman, Bedouin and Egyptians want to be buried here? Could it be that this is the last resting place of Alexander the Great and they wanted to be laid to rest near him? Time will tell.

This site is not as yet open for visiting.

Left: *Allied War Graves at El-Alamein testify to the sacrifice made in World War II*

Left: *Alexander the Great came to the Oasis of Siwa to consult the oracle in 331 BC*

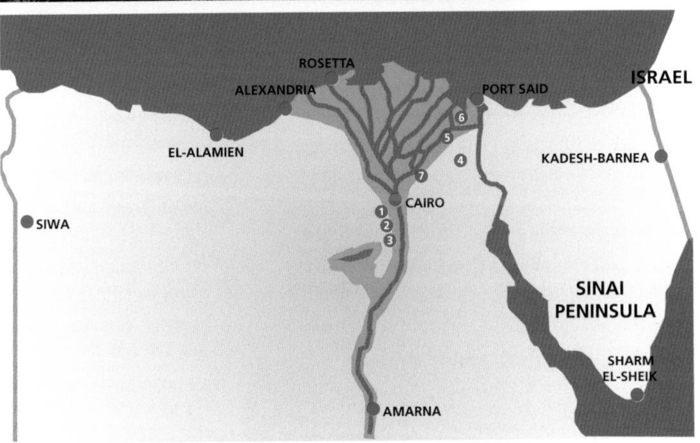

LOCATION OF SITES IN NORTHERN EGYPT

1 GIZA
2 SAQQARA
3 MEMPHIS
4 PITHOM
5 PI RAMESSE/AVARIS
6 TANIS
7 HELIOPOLIS

TRAVEL INFORMATION

Please note that many sites and museums in Egypt do not have websites at present.

Alexandria

Egypt's second largest and most westerly city, and it contains many items of interest including:

Graeco-Roman Museum

5 Sharia al-Mathaf ar-Romani
☎ (03) 486 5820
9.00 am to 5.00 pm daily, 9.00 am to 3.00 pm during Ramadan

This museum contains over 40,000 artefacts from the founding of the city in 331 BC to the Arab conquest of AD 640. Of particular interest is the huge mummified crocodile that was carried in processions honouring the crocodile god Sobek.

Pompey's Pillar

Sharia Ahmoud al-Saweiri

This monument to the emperor Diocletian was once part of the Temple of Serapis.

Bibliotheca Alexandrina

Shabi
☎ (03) 483 999
10.00 am to 7.00 pm
11.00 am to 2.00 pm during Ramadan

Built as a reminder of the great Library of Alexandria and containing many important documents.

El- Alamein

El-Alamein is 105km (66mi) west of Alexandria and is best reached by car or bus, the trains are slow, the station is 2km (1.2mi) from the town. The Italian and German war graves are just off the main highway 4km (2.5mi) to the west of the town, and the British and Commonwealth are indicated by road direction signs. The El-Alamein Museum displays maps of the campaign and one of the most important battles of World War II. It is built in the exact place where the battle took place.
Web address for the Museum www.touregypt.net/featurestories/alemeinmuseum.htm

Although the beach is accessible be aware of the signs regarding unexploded mines!

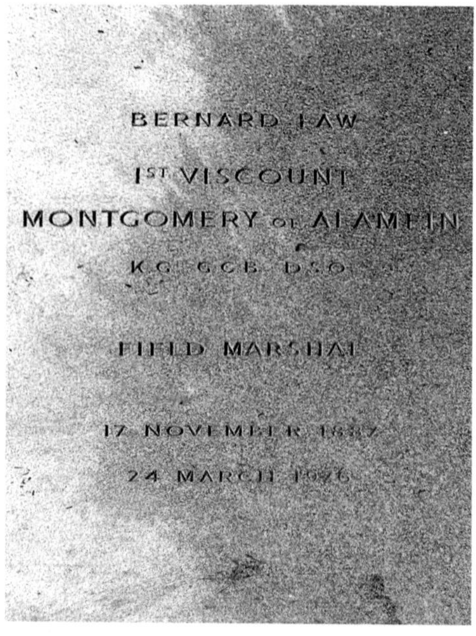

Above: *Montgomery's simple grave in Binstead village churchyard*

Nuweiba

Some have speculated that the crossing may have occurred at Nuweiba on the Red Sea. It appears King Solomon built his navy near here (1 Kings 9:26). If this was the crossing point, the Israelites would have come to Mount Sinai, in Midian, in what is now Saudi Arabia (Galatians 4:25).

Pithom and Ramesses

Tel El-Maskhuta the site of Pithom is 164km (102mi) N of Cairo and Tell ed-Daba/Avaris the site of Ramesses. Due to their location and lack of facilities, they are not normally on the tourist trail.

Siwa Oasis

The desert track follows the caravan route that Alexander the Great used. Travel to this remote and isolated place, which is almost at the Libyan border, is normally by bus/coach from Alexandria or Cairo, or join a tour. Sufficient supplies of water should be taken as the journey is a long one.

Accommodation can be found in hotels or guesthouses or even a tent under the stars.

Tanis (Zoan)

This famous place is located 122km (76mi) NE of Cairo The site contains the ruins of temples and tombs, but many of the treasures have been removed and are on display in the Cairo Museum. See page 49.

Sinai Peninsula

Travel to this area by road from Ismalia or Suez, or by air to Mount Sinai Airport. Scheduled services leave from Cairo.

Mount Sinai and St Catherine's monastery

Located at the foot of Jebel Musa (Sinai?), St Catherine's Monastery was constructed by order of the Emperor Justinian between AD 527 and 565. Many think that this is the site of the well at which Moses watered the flocks for his father-in-law Jethro, where he saw the burning bush and received the Law from God. The monastery houses one of the largest and most important collections of biblical manuscripts in the world. It consists of over 4,500 volumes in Greek, Coptic, Arabic, Armenian, Hebrew, Slavic, Syriac, Georgian and other languages.

Visitor details can be found at Web address www.sinaimonastery.com

Binstead, Hampshire

Field Marshall Bernard Law Montgomery is buried in this small Hampshire village Churchyard not far from Alton. His grave is located behind the Church and is a simple inscribed flat stone. In the Church are many fascinating items including Montgomery's flag of the Order of the Bath that used to hang in the King Henry VII Chapel in Westminster Abbey.

Above: *St Catherine's monastery on Sinai*

③ Stairway to heaven

The pyramid of Cheops is the largest stone building on earth. Before the Battle of the Pyramids on 21 July 1798, Napoleon Bonaparte said to his men: 'Soldiers, from the height of these pyramids, forty centuries look down on you'

At first, some mistakenly thought the Pyramids were the storehouses Joseph built to counter the effects of famine (Genesis 41:49). In fact, the ancient Egyptians built pyramids as tombs for the kings and their queens, and they were buried in pyramids of different shapes and sizes from before the beginning of the Old Kingdom to the end of the Middle Kingdom (see page 114). There are over one hundred of them still existing in ancient Egypt. Despite Hollywood's depictions, the Pyramids were not constructed by slaves, although they may have been involved in hauling the masonry from quarry to building site, but by freemen, usually farmers working together and willingly for their king. As the Nile flooded the land for between three to four months each year, making agriculture impossible, many gave their time to the state, a concept that still exists in many societies where workers pay 25% tax, almost in the same ratio as the ancient Egyptians.

All the Egyptian pyramids are located close to the west bank of the Nile. The largest were built in quick succession, with the three famous ones constructed in the course of only three generations in 70 years. In an age when the majority of dwellings were single story brick built, they represent inconceivable size and incredible weight. The pyramid represented the first land to appear at the beginning of time—a hill called *ben-ben* (see box 'Noah and the ben-ben stone' on page 11). The word 'pyramid' comes from the Greek word *pyramis* which means 'wheat cake', because they reminded the Greeks of wheat

Above: *The Great Pyramid's wonderful construction never ceases to amaze visitors*

Facing page: *The Alabaster Sphinx at Memphis recalls the past glory of the ancient capital of Lower Egypt*

cakes with a pointed top. The ancient Egyptian word for the pyramids was *Mer*.

The Great Pyramid

The Giza Necropolis has been a fashionable tourist destination since antiquity, and was popularized in Hellenistic times (323 to 146 BC) when the Great Pyramid was listed by Antipater of Sido as one of the Seven wonders of the world. Today it is the sole survivor of the ancient wonders.

Pyramids exist in other places, but the ones of Khufu, Khafre, and Menkaure are surely the defining image of ancient Egypt, recognisable the world over. An impression of their solidity and longevity is in the Arab proverb: 'All the world fears time but time fears the pyramids.'

The Great Pyramid is a monumental tomb, constructed for King Khufu (Egyptian), known to the Greeks as Cheops and to the ancient Egyptians as *Ekhet Khufu*, the Horizon of Khufu. Recent work has proposed that the Great Pyramid was orientated so accurately to the stars that a stellar alignment gives the setting of its baselines to around 2478 BC—a similar date to the construction of Stonehenge in England?

Above: *The Great Pyramid rising out of the early morning mist*

When it was built, the Great Pyramid was 146.6m (481ft) high. Over the years, it has lost 10m (32.8ft) of height. It was the tallest structure on earth for forty-three centuries, only to be surpassed in height in the thirteenth century AD by Lincoln Cathedral in England. This immense structure contains approximately 2,300,000 blocks of limestone, with an average weight of two tonnes, and some of the larger ones are between 15 to 30 tonnes. It has been calculated that there are enough blocks in the three famous pyramids to build a 3m (9.84ft) high, by 0.3m (1ft) thick wall around the entire perimeter of France!

Modern calculations have shown that Khufu's builders had to set in place one average size block every two or three minutes in a ten hour day, a staggering achievement. Recent archaeological work has discovered internal ramps that may have been used to transport the blocks up to each ascending course? When the main structure was in place it was then covered with a casing of Turah limestone to smooth its surface and to give it a brilliant white appearance; some of the casing can still be seen on top of Khafre's pyramid. This casing limestone was removed in antiquity by the caliphs of

Left: *The Great Pyramid with Solar Boat Museum*

Cairo in the ninth century AD to construct many buildings. The Victorian traveller Amelia Edwards thought this gave it an unfinished look, as if the workman, 'were coming back tomorrow morning.' Each apex was adorned with electrum, a mixture of gold and silver, which must have been dazzling in the sunlight.

The Great Pyramid slopes at an angle of 51 degrees and 51 minutes, and each side is carefully orientated with one of the cardinal points of the compass. The horizontal cross section of the pyramid is square at any level, with each side measuring 229m (751ft) in length. The maximum error between side lengths is astonishingly less than 0.1%. The interior stones are so well dressed that a thin card will not fit between them. This pyramid covers an area of thirteen acres in its vast space could accommodate St Peter's in Rome, the cathedral of Florence in Milan,and St Paul's and Westminster Abbey in London. Ironically the only known image of Khufu is a tiny limestone statuette just 7.5cm (3inches) tall in the Egyptian Museum in Cairo! (See page 51).

Above: *The Solar Boat Museum contains the vessel discovered in a pit next to the Great Pyramid that may have transported Khufu to his last resting place*

Solar Boat Pit

Five boats in pits are located within the Great Pyramid complex. One was excavated and reassembled using the ancient Egyptian materials: wooden pegs and grass rope. It may well have sailed on the Nile and could have been Khufu's funerary vessel.

Left: The Pyramid of Khafre retains some of its limestone casing near the summit

Now it is displayed in the Solar Boat Museum. A similar boat lies in a nearby pit but has yet to be extracted.

Pyramids of Khafre and Menkaure

Son and grandson of Khufu, their magnificent structures complete the famous site on Giza. The ends of their names *re* reflect the belief in the Sun god Re (or Ra), as does the shape of the buildings. The pyramid complex of King Khafre, or Chephren to the Greeks, is the most complete of all the Giza pyramids. It is built on higher ground than the Great Pyramid and rises at a sharper angle, which gives the illusion that it is larger that the Great Pyramid. When first completed, the pyramid was served by a magnificent mortuary temple which, even in its ruined state, is most impressive. A great stone (diorite) statue of this king is on show in the Egyptian Museum in Cairo. (See page 117).

The pyramid for King Menkaure, to the Greeks Mykerinus, is about half the size of the other two, but is the most perfect in form. Sixteen courses of red granite were used for the lower section, which adds to the strength of the structure. In 1837 Howard Vyse, an English explorer, found a sarcophagus and removed it, but unfortunately it was lost in a storm at sea.

Right: The Pyramid of Menkaure is perfect in form, and despite being half the size of the others on the Giza plateau it is not in any way second-rate

A superb stone triad (schist) statue of this King, protected by Hathor and various local deities, is in the Egyptian Museum in Cairo.

Above: The Great Sphinx standing before the pyramid of Khafre is a magnificent legacy of the Ancient Egyptians' skill in carving stone

The Great Sphinx

Appearing to stand guard over the necropolis at the approach to Khafre's pyramid, the Sphinx is the earliest known monumental sculpture of ancient Egypt. In Arabic the Sphinx is called *Abu Hol*—father of terrors. In Greek, *sphinx* means 'strangler', because in Greek mythology it was a murderous monster that killed those who could not answer her riddles.

This colossal work measures 73.5m (241ft) long and over 20m (65.6ft) high. It may have been carved before the pyramids were constructed, although some scholars think the face could be Khafre's, the builder of the second pyramid; others consider it to be that of Djedefre, a 4th Dynasty Pharaoh. He is wearing the *nemes* or pleated headdress; its shape seems to replicate the hood of a cobra, a snake thought highly of in Ancient Egypt as a danger and a protector, symbols of the king's power. This fact highlights the significance of Aaron's staff being changed into a snake and devouring those of the magicians (Exodus 7:8–12). In his book *Ancient Egypt and the Old Testament*, John D Currid comments: 'The serpent confrontation foreshadowed Yahweh's humiliation of Egypt through the plagues and at the Red Sea. In Exodus 7:12 Aaron's rod swallowed the magicians rods and in Exodus 15:12 the Egyptian Army was swallowed by the Red Sea.'

During the New Kingdom, (see page 114) the Sphinx was regarded as a manifestation of the sun god. Between its paws is the dream stela of Tuthmosis IV, where he claims the sun god appeared to him in a dream and would make him king if he cleared away the sand from the Sphinx.

It is incredible to think of the many great names which would have looked into the face of the Sphinx including: Abraham, Jacob, Joseph, Moses, Aaron, Jeremiah, Joseph, Mary and the infant Jesus from Bible times. Others from history include such diverse characters as Alexander the Great, Caesar Augustus,

Saladin, Napoleon Bonaparte, Florence Nightingale and Agatha Christie.

Surrounding the famous pyramids are much smaller ones belonging to queens and princesses, and the mastaba tombs of high officials, several of which can now be visited.

Battle of the Pyramids

Napoleon fought a military engagement on 21 July 1798 on the west bank of the Nile River, when his army of 25,000 faced perhaps 40,000 Egyptians led by Murad Bey. The Egyptians were concentrated with the ancient pyramids of Giza on their left flank, but when the French stormed the Egyptian camp they dispersed their army with only 300 casualties to themselves. Even though the battle was a rout, it had not been the comprehensive victory Napoleon had hoped for because too many of the enemy escaped.

Top: *The face of the Great Sphinx reveals some of the ancient colouring on the Nemes headdress*

Above: *The souvenir stalls near the Pyramids offer a great range of items to attract the tourist*

William Flinders Petrie

Born on 3 June 1853 in Charlton, Kent, Petrie is called the father of Egyptology and is one of the pioneers of the modern archaeological method. He was raised in a devout Christian household and his father belonged to the Plymouth Brethren and his mother to the Anglican Church. By the age of eight he was being tutored in French, Latin and Greek and was encouraged from childhood to pursue archaeological interests. Petrie travelled to Egypt in 1880 and, when surveying the Great Pyramid at Giza, he applied the same methods he had used at Stonehenge in England. Returning home, he wrote articles and so impressed Amelia Edwards, journalist and patron of the Egypt Exploration Fund (now the Egypt Exploration Society), that she appointed him to her chair of Egyptology at University College, London. He returned to the Middle East and began excavating in Egypt, where he discovered the Merneptah Stele which contains the earliest known reference to Israel, (see page 51). He also surveyed a group of tombs in the Wadi al-Rababah (biblical Hinnom) in Jerusalem.

***Above:** Sir (William Matthew) Flinders Petrie painted by George Frederic Watts*

His simple lifestyle, in which food hygiene was never a priority, became the stuff of legend and T.E. Lawrence (Lawrence of Arabia), who was one of Petrie's students, commented that 'a Petrie dig is a thing with a flavour of its own.' Flinders Petrie was knighted for services to British archaeology and Egyptology in 1923 and died on 29 July 1942 in Jerusalem; he was buried in the Protestant cemetery located near the Zion gate with his gravestone facing the rising sun. (See *Travel through Israel* in this series, page 109).

***Left:** The few remains on view make it difficult to realise how magnificent the city of Memphis must have been*

Memphis

Memphis, located on the west side of the River Nile just south of modern day Cairo, is believed by some Egyptologists to have been founded by King Menes, a First Dynasty Pharaoh, in about 3,000 BC and it became the capital in about 2,600 BC. Its name is derived from the Egyptian, *men-nefer-pepi*, the name given to the pyramid of King Pepi I.

The Memphite version of the creation myth states that Ptah brought the universe into being by conceiving it in his heart (compare Hebrews 11:3), and all created things lived when Ptah declared their names (see Genesis 2:19). Memphis would have been well known to Joseph and is the likely centre of his work as vizier of Egypt (Genesis 41:40). It is possibly the location of the first confrontation between Moses, Aaron and Pharaoh (Exodus 5:1–2) and the location of the confrontation with Pharaoh's court magicians Jannes and Jambres (see 2 Timothy 3:8 and Exodus 7:8–13).

Colonies of foreigners established themselves here, including Jews after the Babylonian destruction of Jerusalem (Jeremiah 44:1). Hosea, the biblical prophet, warned that any Jews who escaped the judgement of God would be buried here (Hosea 9:6). A stone stela of Pharaoh Hophra, who was turned over to his enemies (Jeremiah 44:30), is here in Memphis. An obelisk to this king stands on top of a marble white elephant outside the Pantheon in Rome. It is probable that Joseph, Mary and the infant Jesus would have come here after the flight from the wrath of King Herod (Matthew 2:13–15). Joseph as a carpenter/builder would have been able to find ample employment in this busy place until the time came for them to return to Nazareth,

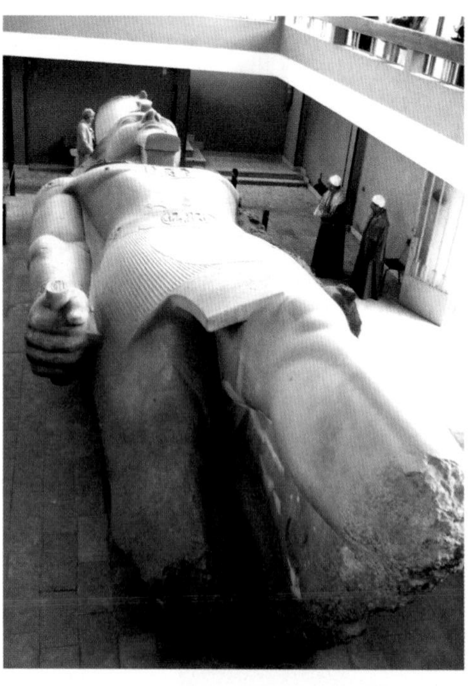

***Above:** The colossal fallen statue of Ramesses II at Memphis reveals fulfilled Bible prophecy, see Ezekiel 30:13*

Right: *A close up of the fallen statue of Ramesses II at Memphis still exudes power and majesty*

(Matthew 2:19–23). The ruined state of Memphis is testimony to prophecy fulfilled (Ezekiel 29:15 and 30:13). It is to be hoped that future large-scale excavations will reveal something of the splendour of this former capital of Lower Egypt.

On/Heliopolis

On was the cult of the sun, centred on the city named in Egyptian as Iunu, known to the Greeks as Heliopolis 'city of the sun.' Its name recurs more frequently than that of any other earthly place in the religious literature of ancient Egypt; it was the model for Thebes in the New Kingdom, and probably of Akhenaten's new city, Akhetaten (see Tel el Armana page 66). Few tourists visit this important site as there is little to see; Strabo, the Greek geographer writing about 24 BC, found the great temples ruined and ready to be used as a source for embellishing the cities of Alexandria and Rome. Joseph's wife came from this city (Genesis 41:45 and 46:20) and he was familiar with this place; it was the likely location where he lived with Potiphar, the Egyptian *pa di pa Ra*, 'the one whom the god Ra has given' (Genesis 37:36). This city would be the place of judgement and death (Ezekiel 30:17). During the Middle Ages, pilgrims visited the church near the site to view the tree in whose shade, supposedly, the Holy Family rested after escaping from King Herod (Matthew 2:15).

Above: *The solitary column at On makes it difficult to imagine the splendour of this city*

Nasr City, Cairo

President Anwar al-Sadat was assassinated on 6 October 1981 during the annual victory parade in Cairo celebrating the campaigns during the 1973 Egypt/Israeli war. He was buried under the Unknown Soldier Memorial in Cairo.

Top: Former President Anwar Sadat is buried under the Memorial to the Unknown Soldier

Above: The Step pyramid at Saqqara, is the oldest monumental stone structure in the world

Saqqara

This complex and important site contains the earliest stone monumental building in the world. Saqqara contains tombs from every period of Egyptian history including the step pyramid of King Zoser (or Djoser). The king commanded his chief minister Imhotep (considered to be the father of medicine) to build him a magnificent tomb. He decided to construct six mastabas (see Glossary on page 112) in decreasing size on top of each other, to create a stunning spectacle. The pyramid is built of locally quarried clayey sandstone of poor quality and it is 60m (200ft) high and has a base measurement of 121m (397ft) by 109m (358ft). It became the prototype for all subsequent pyramids, and is often thought to have been created as a stairway on which the king's immortal soul could ascend to the heavens; there he would take his place alongside the sun and the other gods.

Serapeum

A series of catacombs, created for the burial of the sacred Apis bull. These bulls were singled out as manifestations of the Memphite god Ptah. They had particular markings, black with a white spot on the forehead and another near the tail, and were left to roam free in the grounds of Ptah's temple at Memphis.

This extensive burial chamber contains twenty-five massive granite sarcophagi, some weighing up to 80 tons. All but one had all been robbed in antiquity. The Louvre in Paris has the solid gold statue found here and the Agricultural Museum in Cairo has the surviving mummified bull.

The Israelites were in Egypt for 430 years and imbibed many of the thought processes and practices from there, so that it did not take them long to revert to type when they constructed a golden calf in the wilderness, not dissimilar to the worship of the Apis and other bulls (Exodus 32:4). Bull worship was also a curse to them in the Promised Land (1 Kings 12:28 to 29, 2 Kings 10:29).

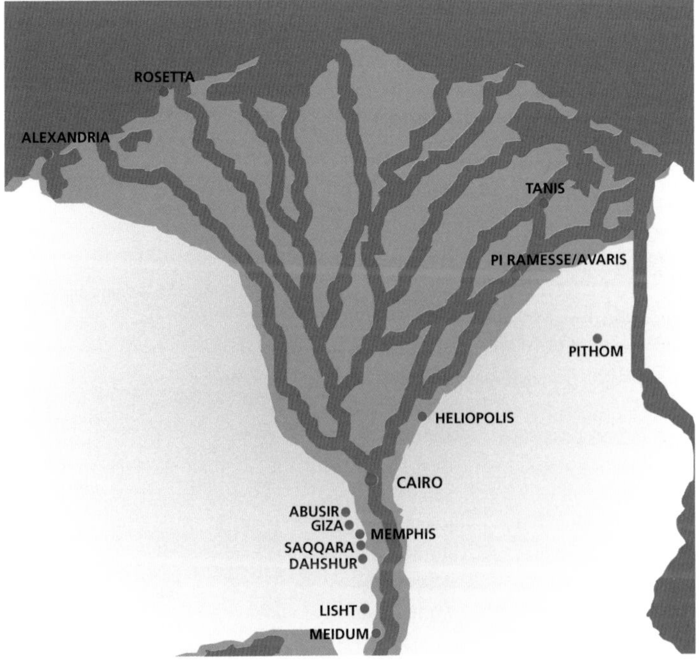

LOCATION OF CITIES AND PYRAMIDS IN THE DELTA

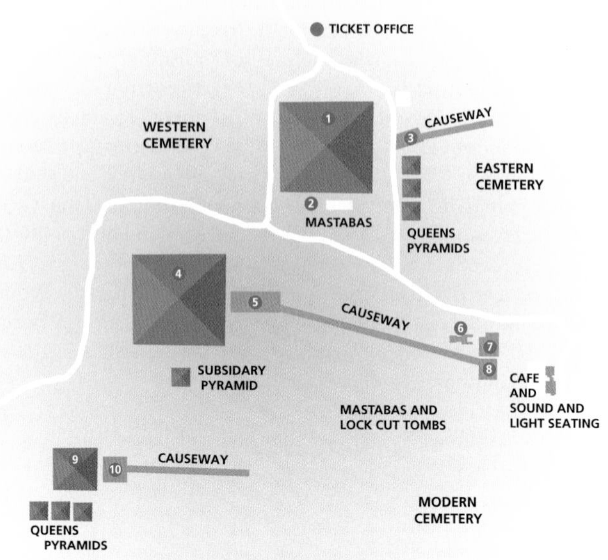

THE LOCATION OF ANCIENT STRUCTURES AT GIZA

1 PYRAMID OF KHUFU
2 BOAT MUSEUM
3 FUNERARY TEMPLE
4 PYRAMID OF KHAFRE
5 FUNERARY TEMPLE
6 GREAT SPHINX
7 TEMPLE OF THE SPHINX
8 VALLEY TEMPLE OF KHAFRE
9 PYRAMID OF MENKAURE
10 FUNERARY TEMPLE

TRAVEL INFORMATION

Giza Plateau

Located 10km (6mi) SW of Cairo.

For preservation purposes each of the famous pyramids is closed in rotation. The ticket office will advise as to availability. Also, numbers may be restricted so it is best to check in advance if an internal visit is anticipated. Since the 1980s it has been illegal to climb the pyramids, because previous generations of tourist have left unsightly graffiti at the top. Also, this move has prevented injury and even death to climbers. On the South side of the Great Pyramid is the Boat Museum, which is well worth a visit.

Each evening a spectacular Sound and Light show is performed in different languages, check beforehand to find out the timings and language required.

Above: *Camel rides can be taken at the Pyramids*

Mena house Oberoi (Hotel)

Mena House Oberoi,
Cairo,
Pyramids' Road, Giza,
Cairo, Egypt
E-mail: Mohit.nirula@oberoihotels.com
☎ +20 2 33 77 3222
☎ +20 2 33 76 6644
🖷 +20 2 33 77 5411
🖷 +20 2 33 76 7777

If time permits a cool refreshing drink here in the shadow of the Pyramids is an excellent way to freshen up after a visit or to conclude a day's sightseeing, as those great structures take on the colour of the setting sun. Located in forty acres of jasmine-scented gardens, this palatial hotel in the shadow of the Pyramids has enchanted guests since 1869. Mena House has played host to kings and emperors, heads of state and celebrities. Here in 1943, Churchill and Roosevelt discussed the plans for operation Overlord, the invasion of Europe.

Dr Ragab's Papyrus Institute

Corniche al-Nil, Doqqi

Housed on a boat not far from the Cairo Sheraton, this is a good place to purchase replica papyrus, also includes a demonstration as to how the papyrus plant is turned into writing material.

Gezira Palace hotel

Saraya El-Gezira Street
☎ 00 20 2 2728 3000
www.Marriott.co.uk

Agatha Christie stayed in this hotel when visiting Cairo.

Memphis

The ancient ruins are 47km (29mi) south of Cairo. The great Statue of Ramesses II is well worth seeing.

On

Heliopolis is located 12km (7.5mi) NE of Cairo; this is not to be confused with the Cairo district of New Heliopolis. Only scanty remains are available to see but it is hoped that future excavation work will reveal more of this important site.

Saqqara

This vast necropolis lies 20km (12.5mi) from Cairo. There are many other fascinating structures and tombs in the area, but if time is limited then it is best to focus on the Step Pyramid.

Serapeum

The Apis Bulls were buried here in huge stone sarcophagi. Opening times can be obtained locally. It could be helpful to take a torch and maybe a cardigan as it is much cooler inside than out in the desert.

Agricultural Museum

Off Wizaret al-Ziraa,
Doqqi, Cairo

This museum contains a mummified bull from the Serapeum as well as examples of ancient farming equipment and bread through the ages.

The Coptic Museum Cairo

Mary George St. Old Cairo
☎ 3639742
www.copticmuseum.gov.eg

Founded in 1910 AD to trace the history of Christianity in Egypt.

Right: *The Pyramids seen from the Mena House hotel*

④ 'Wonderful things'

The Egyptian Museum is a true Aladdin's cave of treasures. Gold, precious stones, exquisite jewellery, statues, inscriptions, papyrus, and the mummified remains of some of the greatest kings in history all lie within its walls

Due to the large number of artefacts in the Egyptian Museum in Cairo only a few of the most significant are highlighted in this chapter. The entrance room contains a cast of the Rosetta Stone which was so instrumental in deciphering the hieroglyphic script (see page 21). The original is in the British Museum in London. The Ground Floor houses the gigantic statues of Amenhotep III and his principal wife Queen Tiye. Amenhotep III reigned at the time Israel were consolidating their position in the Promised Land. On the ground floor are many artefacts dealing with the reign of his son, the heretic Pharaoh Akhenaten (see page 65), including a defaced coffin that may have been his.

Ground Floor Gallery 21. *Sesostris III*. Joseph probably served as vizier to this king

Ground Floor Room 42. *Khafre Room*. Large statue of the builder of the second Pyramid at Giza.

Ground Floor Room 43. *Narmer Palette*. This schist palette (c.3,100 BC) commemorates the victories of Narmer, whom tradition identifies with King Menes the unifier of Upper and Lower Egypt.

Ground Floor Room 43. *King Zoser*. This painted life-size limestone statue is of Zoser, the builder of the Step Pyramid at Saqqara.

Above: *Cairo's Egyptian Museum is one of the great museums in the world*

Facing page: *The exquisite gold mask of Tutankhamun is a magnificent tribute to the skill of ancient Egyptian jewellers. The false beard is upturned to denote death and the ears are pierced for ear rings.*

temple in Thebes by the archaeologist Flinders Petrie. This large stone stela, 3.18m (10.4ft) tall by 1.63m (5.34ft) wide and 31cm (1ft) thick, has been meticulously scrutinized and analysed by scholars, more than any Old Testament text outside the Bible, because it contains the earliest mention of Israel in Egyptian records, to date. The inscription is a poetic eulogy to pharaoh Merneptah (see page 57), who ruled after Ramesses II. The important line says: 'Israel is laid waste, its seed is not'. If Israel was an established entity in Canaan in 1210 BC, as the Merneptah Stela implies, then the people were already settled in the Promised Land and an early date for the Exodus is favourable. It may be significant that this stela was originally placed in the mortuary temple of Amenhotep III (1390–1352 BC) at Thebes and may have been carved then, which would mean the early date for the Exodus becomes more significant if Merneptah re-carved part of the stela and replaced the name of Amenhotep with his own.

Ground Floor Gallery 47. Large triad of *Menkaure*, the builder of the third pyramid of Giza showing him with the goddess Hathor and local deities. (See page 116 for the dates for Egyptian kings).

Ground Floor Room 13. Israel is no more.
One of the most important artefacts in the Museum is the *Merneptah stele* discovered in 1896 in Merneptah's mortuary

Above: *Top of the Narma Palatte depicting King Narma unifying the two lands of Upper and Lower Egypt c. 3100 BC*

Below: *Part of life-sized statues of Rahotep and his wife Nofret (Room 32)*

Upper Floor, Room 2. Furniture of *Queen Hetepheres.* Many of these items help in giving the background to the Old Testament. Note especially the joints at the top of her canopy; they are similar to the joints used in the Tabernacle constructed in the Wilderness.

Upper Floor Room 3. *Ceremonial Axe of Ahmose* He may have been the king who ordered the death of the Hebrew Firstborn (Exodus 1:16).

Upper Floor Hall 48. *King Khufu.* A very small statue of the builder of the Great Pyramid.

Upper floor, many rooms. *Tutankhamun's treasure.* The wonderful items found in the young king's tomb not only testify to the amazing riches of Egypt but also help to illustrate the ambiance of the Bible. Bezalel, Oholiab and many other craftsmen were chosen to build the Tabernacle and its furnishings, and undoubtedly they would have learnt much by watching or assisting the Egyptians, (Exodus 31:1–11).

A few of the thousands of items are listed below.

Carrying boxes. There are a number of examples of boxes including the excellent one found in the treasury with a carving of Anubis sitting on top. The Ark of the Covenant (1.22m x 0.76m x 0.76 m) would have been larger in size to the portable redwood funerary chest, (0.83m x 0.635m x 0.6m) but the carrying poles are suggestive of the way the Ark was handled (Exodus 25:15).

Above: *The Merneptah stela contains the earliest known reference to Israel*

Below: *A miniature statue of King Khufu the builder of the Great Pyramid*

Thrones and Footstalls. An exquisite throne covered in gold depicts Tutankhamun with his queen Ankhsenamun under the rays of the Aten disk. The enemies of Egypt were under the control of the king, each people-group was carved onto a footstall, so when the king placed his feet on it, all realised he was the supreme controller and governor in the world (See Psalm 110:1).

Shrines. These fit one inside the other and are a magnificent example of ancient craftsmanship.

Coffins. Each of the three coffins that enclosed the mummy of the king have different faces, perhaps indicating that they were intended for other people, but the suddenness of Tutankhamun's death caught the undertakers unawares. The breathtaking inner coffin, of beaten gold and beautifully cast, is 1.88m (6.16ft) long and weighs 110.4kg (296lbs). The Israelites used something similar in the construction of the atonement cover on the Ark of the Covenant (Exodus 25:17 to 18).

Above: *This portable redwood funerary chest and carrying poles from the treasure of Tutankhamun approximates to the size and transportation of the biblical Ark of the Covenant*

Below: *A wall painting showing priests carrying a chest at Abydos is reminiscent of the Israelites transporting the Ark of the Covenant*

Gold Mask. Superbly modelled, it is without parallel as a masterpiece of the Egyptian metalworkers' craft.

Chariot. Tutankhamun's chariot is on display. The Museum has other examples of chariots and models of soldiers. The use of chariots was widespread among the Hittites in Anatolia, the Hyksos in Syro-Palestine, and among the Kassites in Mesopotamia. The size, organization, and highly disciplined personnel of the Egyptian army made whatever armament the Israelites had ineffective (Exodus 13:18). Egyptian military chariots of the 15th century BC had a wooden frame partially covered with leather and two wheels with each wheel having four spokes. This was harnessed to two horses. At night, the wheels had to be removed and the chariot frame laid on its side to prevent warping caused by temperature change. On entering the Promised Land the Israelites encountered new and terrifying chariots (Judges 1:19).

Royal Mummy rooms

This unique display makes it high on the list of visitor's priorities.

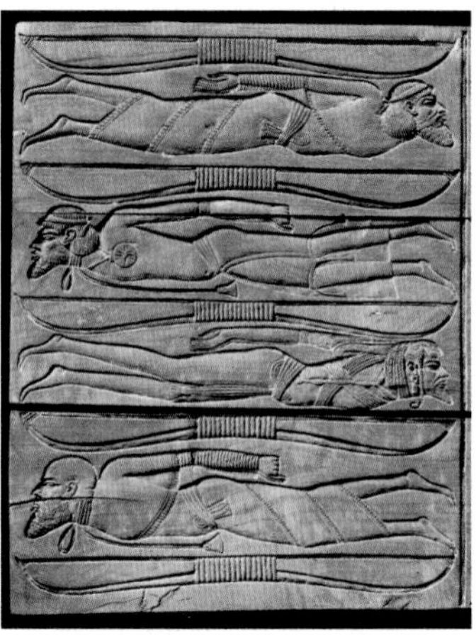

Above: *Egypt's enemies were represented as nine bows. Five bows can be seen here on part of Tutankhamun's footstool, above Canaanites and Asiatics. The king would ceremonially place his feet on his defeated enemy (see Joshua 10:24).* *©Robert Harding/Robert Harding*

Below: *Carved heads of Egypt's enemies in the grounds of the Cairo Museum*

Ancient Egyptians desired to have their names spoken after death, but caution has to be exercised in being dogmatic about the identity of some of the human remains, as the recent examination of the mummy of 'Tuthmosis I' has shown;

Mummification

The body of the deceased was taken to the ibw 'Place of Purification,' where it was stripped and washed whilst prayers were said over it by priests. Next came the per nefer 'House of Beauty' where the mummification took place. The chief embalmer wore a jackal mask in order to imitate Anubis, the jackal-headed god of embalming. St Augustine in his confessions makes mention of Anubis the 'barking deity'.

The cheapest method was to wash the body, soak it in natron (dry sodium salts), then bandage and bury it in a cheap coffin. The most expensive procedure involved the embalmers inserting a long thin strip of metal into the left nostril breaking the nasal bone, before breaking up the brain and washing it out with a mixture of aromatic spices and wine. A sharp flint knife make a long incision in the left abdomen, (similar ones were used in Joshua 5:2) so that the liver, lungs, stomach and intestines could be removed and mummified separately, an embalming plate would have covered the incision. The viscera were then embalmed and placed in four separate jars with different head-shaped stoppers imitating the four sons of Horus.

The embalmers left the heart and kidneys in place, the heart was considered to be the centre of all intellect and emotions. The corpse was placed in natron for forty days, and then washed off and oiled. Amulets were included in the wrapping process; the completed mummy was placed in a coffin, then into a sarcophagus in the tomb. Royal mummies received the best treatment and naturally the embalmers were justly proud of their work, and existing examples show how remarkably gifted they were. The entire process from death to burial took seventy days, and Jacob and Joseph would have been prepared after this fashion, (Genesis 50:2–3 and 26).

instead of being an old king it is that of a young man killed by an arrow. It is not possible to know which mummies the museum will have on display, though the following are normally shown.

Seqenenre Tao II (1560–1546 BC). Responding to a severe insult from the Hyksos this king began the war of independence, unsuccessfully as he suffered a violent death before being hastily embalmed. He was 1.7m (5.57ft) tall, and the face has six terrible wounds inflicted by spear, mace and axe, and in his death agony he has bitten through his tongue! If an early date is taken for the Exodus then his younger son Ahmose, was probably the king who ordered the death of the Hebrew boys, (Exodus 1:15–16). Ahmose's mummy lies in the Luxor museum.

Tuthmosis II (1492–1479 BC). Tuthmosis could be the king who wanted to kill Moses (Exodus 2:15), he was 1.68m (5.51ft) tall but his mummy is in a poor state. This king, who died when he was about 30 years old, had married his half sister Hatshepsut, who bore him a daughter. Another minor wife, Iset, gave birth to the future Tuthmosis III.

Hatshepsut (1479–1457 BC). This incredible woman was strong willed and gifted, with unprecedented political determination. On the death of her husband Tuthmosis II, she usurped the throne ahead of the young Tuthmosis III. She assumed the masculine titles of kingship in the seventh year of her reign and was portrayed as a man. An early date for the Exodus means she would have grown up in the court of Egypt when Moses was educated there (Acts 7:22). She probably oppressed the Hebrews, for it is not unknown for women to be persecutors (1 Kings 21:9 and 2 Chronicles 22:10), and it is possible that her passing saw the beginning of the deliverance of the Hebrews (Exodus 2:15 and 23). Her mummy, discovered by Howard Carter in 1903, was only identified on 27 June 2007 when a fragment of a tooth with her cartouche on it, in the Museum's possession, was shown to be hers. Hatshepsut was about 50 years of age at death, obese with huge breasts; she suffered from diabetes and bone cancer. Tuthmosis III surprisingly started to deface some of her monuments in the forty-second year of his reign (c.1437 BC). Could this be linked to the Exodus, perhaps blaming her for being associated with Moses? Hatshepsut was omitted from king lists because her reign was too disgraceful to mention.

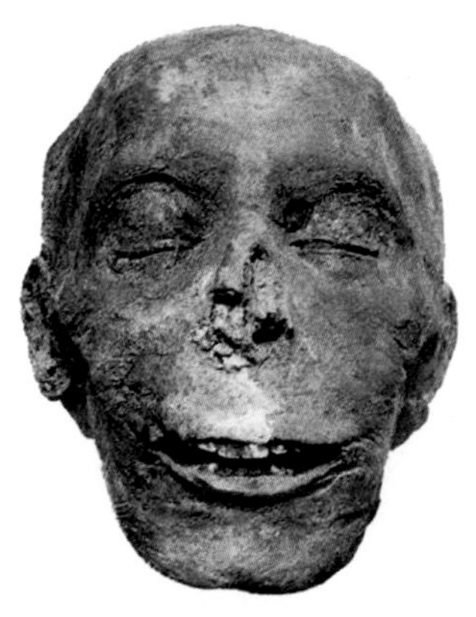

Above: *The mummified head of Tuthmosis III, Egypt's greatest warrior and possibly the man who was confronted by Moses and Aaron?*

Tuthmosis III (1479 to 1425 BC). Tuthmosis III was Egypt's greatest warrior, sometimes referred to as the Napoleon of Egypt. He turned his kingdom into an empire, reigned for 53 years and 11 months and soon after the death of Hatshepsut (year 23 of his reign) he opened up his eastern campaign which included the dramatic victory at the 'miserable city of Megiddo'. He was 1.61m (5.28ft) tall and the shoulders, chest arms, legs and feet are covered with papules (unidentified lumps) of different sizes (Exodus 9:10). Damage inflicted by tomb robbers means his mummy is in a poor state of preservation. It is likely that he opposed Moses and Aaron (Exodus 9:15–16, and Romans 9:17). In proscribing the monuments of Hatshepsut (see above) Tuthmosis was rewriting history by trying to reaffirm maat (order, balance and harmony) because her reign was perceived as being out of balance with Egyptian history (resulting in the Exodus?).

Amenhotep II (1427 to 1400 BC). This king was an athletic but brutal man, who often boasted of his great prowess as a soldier and hunter. Victor

Loret found his body in a pink granite sarcophagus, he was 1.67m (5.47ft) tall. Like his predecessor, the skin of the thorax, shoulders, arms, legs and feet are covered with papules of different sizes (Exodus 9:10). Joshua entered the Promised Land and started the process of conquest in 1406 BC, (Joshua 1:11) during his reign. Although it may be significant that in Year 9 of his reign after campaigning in Palestine, reaching as far as the Sea of Galilee he never went to war again, could something have happened to the army (Exodus 14:28)? His mummy is not on show at the time of writing.

Tuthmosis IV (1400 to 1390 BC). This king had placed the dream stela between the paws of the famous Sphinx at Giza, detailing the sphinx's promise to make him king if he cleared it of sand. He was reigning when Joshua began the conquest of the Promised Land.

Amenhotep III (1390 to 1352 BC). Amenhotep became king at 13 years of age and married Queen Tiye; he claimed divinity when the construction of the Luxor Temple began. He was probably the wealthiest of all the Pharaohs and the Amarna letters were written to him and his son Akhenaten (see page 66). His mummy is in a poor state of preservation with the head being detached from the body, and he also suffered serious dental problems with many cavities, abundant tartar and a large abscess. This mummy is not on show at the time of writing.

Seti I (1291 to 1278 BC). Seti's face is the best preserved of any of the Royal mummies so far discovered. A late date for the Exodus means he could have been the Pharaoh of the oppression.

Ramesses II (1279 to 1213 BC). Whatever else maybe said about this man, he certainly deserves the title of Ramesses the Great,

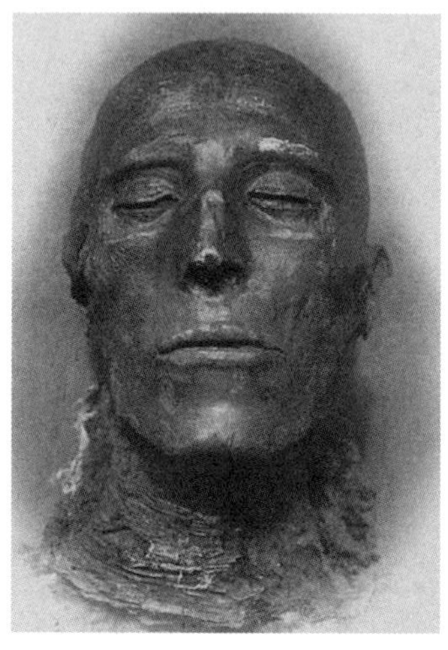

Above: *The mummified face of King Seti I. His face is the best preserved of all the Royal Mummies*

Below: *The regal profile of Ramesses II*

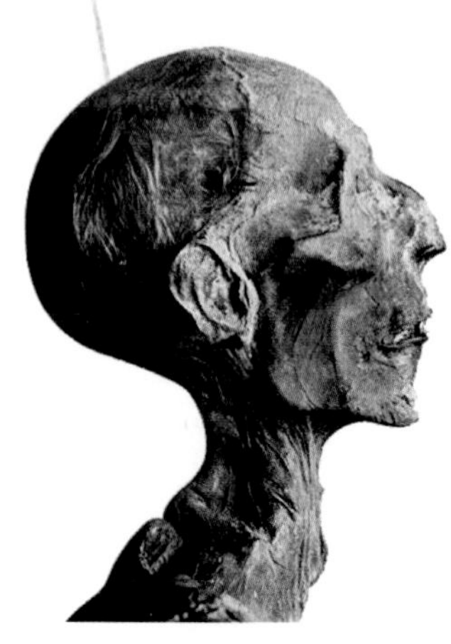

Above: Ramesses II is called Ramesses the Great because of his many achievements. For sixty years he presided over an era of peace and prosperity that no other Egyptian king enjoyed; subsequent kings took his name in the vain hope that they would emulate his achievements. His monuments can be found in every corner of the Egyptian Empire

for the extraordinary length and achievements of his reign. At 1.733m (5.8ft) Ramesses was tall for a dynastic Egyptian, and recent examination reveals battle scar tissue on his skin. A late date for the Exodus means he could have been the Pharaoh whose army perished in the Red Sea

Merneptah (1213 to 1204 BC). The thirteenth son of Ramesses II. Great excitement was generated when this mummy was first unwrapped, because it appeared to be covered in salt, and therefore some thought he must have been the Pharaoh who perished in the Red Sea! However it was soon realised that the light colour of his skin was caused by prolonged contact with bags of salt used during the embalming process. The body is of an elderly person 1.72m (5.64ft) tall, who had suffered from serious dental problems. See Merneptah Stele page 50.

Ramesses III (1186 to 1154 BC). This is the last of the great kings to rule over Egypt. He defended his country from the massive invasion by the Sea peoples and among that group were the Philistines who eventually settled on the lower western part of Israel and became a thorn in the flesh of the Israelites (Joshua 13:2). According to the Harem Conspiracy Papyrus in Turin Museum, this king suffered a violent death due to a conspiracy being engineered by a minor consort; all conspirators were executed (see the screaming man overleaf). The face of Ramesses III was used as the basis for the make up of Boris Karloff, in the 1932 movie *The Mummy*.

This was the first Hollywood movie where a mummy-monster is brought back to life to terrorise the living.

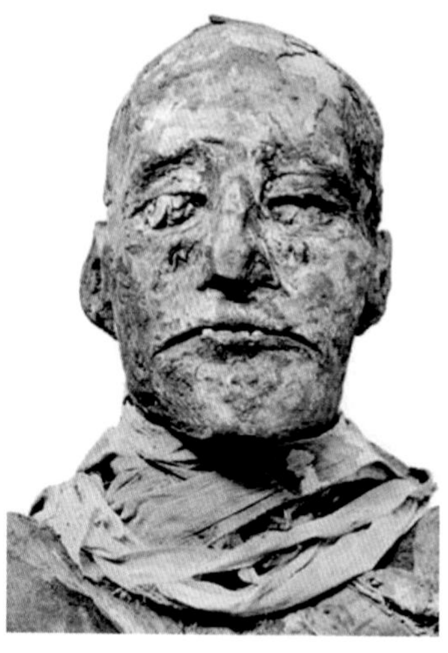

The screaming man. His mouth open in a soundless scream, the stomach painfully contracted, the arms tightly bound down by the sides and the legs tied together. He had been wrapped in a goat/sheep skin, which rendered him ritually unclean, and great care seems to have been taken over the mummification process to ensure that he would not enter the afterlife. But why? Recent studies identify him as the rebel Prince Penterwere, who may have been allowed to poison himself rather then being impaled for treason against Ramesses III. This hideous act was probably carried out in the Great Prison at Thebes, where Joseph had previously been incarcerated (Genesis 39:20). He was 1.7m (5.8ft) tall and about 40 years of age at death.

More mummies. Throughout the museum there are also many animal mummies including crocodiles, dogs, cats, birds and snakes all testifying not only to the remarkable skill of the embalmers but also to the religious beliefs of the Egyptians

The sign of life

All over the museum are countless examples of the *Ankh*, considered by some to be the crooked cross or satanic symbol, although the ancient Egyptians would have been amazed by that assumption. The shape probably represents a sandal with the loop being the heel of the sandal, the cross

Top: *The face of Ramesses III modelled by Boris Karloff in the film 'The Mummy'*

Above: *The Ankh is the ancient Egyptian sign of life*

piece the strap across the foot and the long piece the strap that goes down and ends up between the toes. The ancient Egyptians called part of the sandal *nkh* (exact pronunciation unknown), because this word was composed of the same consonants as the word 'life'. The sign to represent that particular part of the sandal was also used to write the word 'life'. The *ankh* word was used for mirrors from at least the Middle Kingdom onward, and many mirrors were shaped in the form of an *ankh* sign. In fact, the *ankh* sign in ancient Egypt seems to have transcended illiteracy, being understood even to those who could not read. Hence, we even find it as a craftsman's mark on pottery vessels. As the Christian era eclipsed Egypt's religion, the sign was adapted by the Coptic Church as their unique form of a cross, known as the *crux ansata*.

Above: *The mummified head of Ahmose*

Below: *The coffin of Amenhotep I*

A possible sequence for the Exodus

Above: The mummified head of Amenhotep II

The Bible does not name the kings who were involved in the Exodus; however, it may be possible to reconstruct the likely scenario using biblical dating and archaeological work. The Bible speaks of a great part of Pharaoh's army perishing in the Red Sea, but it does not explicitly state that the king was drowned (Exodus14: 23, 15:4, Psalm 78:53 and Psalm 106:11).

Note: A new chronology of the ancient world has been proposed in recent years but has not found general acceptance. For a reasoned response to the new chronology see, The *Third Intermediate Period in Egypt* by K. A. Kitchen, 2004, ISBN 0–85668–298–5.

Ahmose (1550 to 1525 BC) removed the hated Hyksos from the Land and probably ordered the death of the Hebrew boys (Exodus 1:8–22). Moses was born c.1526 BC.

Amenhotep I (1525 to 1504 BC) Or this king may have ordered their deaths (Exodus 1:8-22).

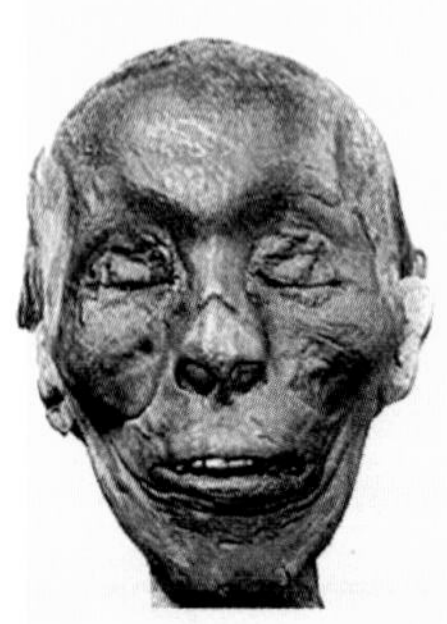

Above: The mummified head of Tuthmosis II

Tuthmosis II (1492 to 1479 BC). In his reign Moses fled from Egypt c1486 BC.

Tuthmosis III (1479 to1425 BC). Moses returned to Egypt and the Exodus took place in 1446 BC.

Exodus 12:41 states that the Exodus was 430 years after Jacob had settled in Egypt (in 1876 BC). That would bring us to a date for the Exodus of 1446 BC. Similarly, 1 Kings 6:1 states the 480 years before Solomon built the Temple in Jerusalem. Solomon built the Temple in the fourth year of his reign which was 966 BC. 480 years before this brings us again to 1446 BC.

Amenhotep II (1427 to 1400 BC). Joshua started the occupation of the Promised Land during his reign.

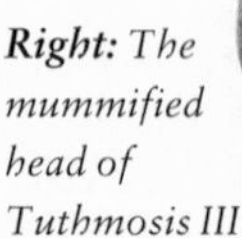

Right: The mummified head of Tuthmosis III

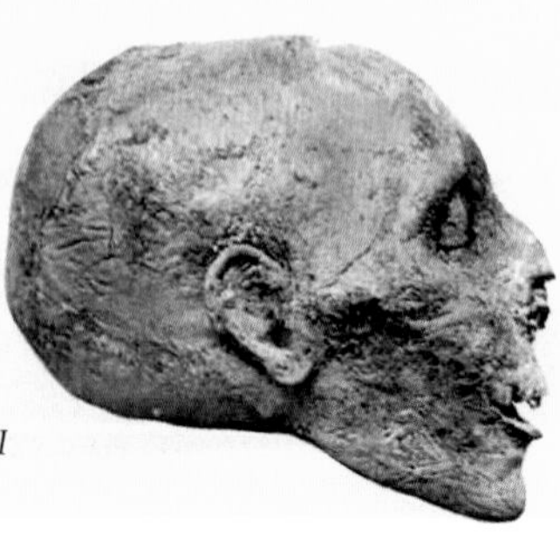

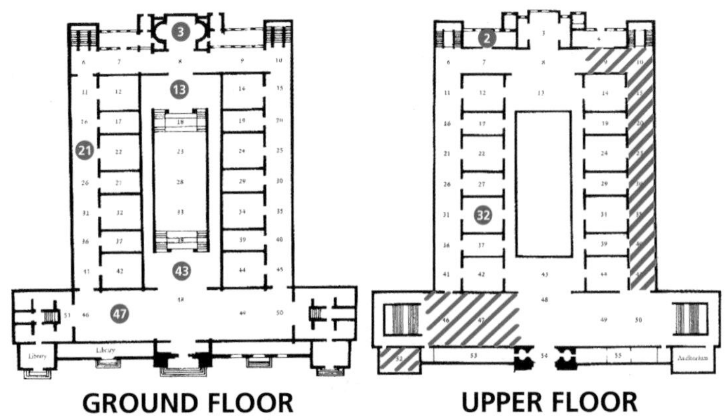

LOCATION OF THE MUSEUMS COLLECTION

You will find pieces mentioned in the book in the following rooms

GROUND FLOOR

3 AMARNA PERIOD PIECES
13 MERNEPTAH STELE
21 SESOSTRIS III
43 NARMA PALATE AND KING ZOSER
47 TRIAD OF MENKAURE

UPPER FLOOR

2 QUEEN HETEPHERES FURNITURE
32 NOFRET & RAHOTEP

SHADED RED AREA
TUTANKHAMUN TREASURE
SHADED GREEN AREA
ROYAL MUMMY ROOMS

TRAVEL INFORMATION

Egyptian Museum

Midan Tahir, Cairo
☎ (02) 578 2448
www.egyptianmuseum.gov.eg

Separate admission charge for the Royal Mummy Room

For further information regarding the Royal Mummies oi.uchicago.edu/research/pubs/nn/win95_wente.html

New Museum

A new museum is being constructed near the Pyramids to house Tutankhamun's treasures and the Royal Mummies, but this will not open for a few years.

Below: The Egyptian Museum, Cairo

5 The horizon of the sun

Small clay tablets and fragments of papyrus may not be everyone's idea of treasure, but many of these documents discovered in the past one hundred and fifty years have not only enlightened history, but have also caused great controversy

The 14th century BC was a period of vibrant cultural relations and political activity throughout the Middle East and the eastern Mediterranean. Exotic merchandise was widely traded and triggered distinctive styles that have helped archaeologists discover the extent of international trade and relationships. But other periods of history have also become more accessible due to startling discoveries.

Nag Hammadi

In 1945 a badly damaged collection of Gnostic books was discovered at Nag Hammadi on the east bank of the Nile in Upper Egypt. The Gnostics were an heretical 'Christian' cult that denied, among much else, the deity of Christ and the reality of his death and resurrection; they believed they had secret knowledge, hence their name which comes from the Greek word *gnosis*, 'knowledge'. Three of the books in what is known as the Nag Hammadi Library are: The Gospel of Thomas, a collection of 114 supposed sayings of Jesus, the Gospel of Philip which is full of obscure and mysterious sayings and claims that the world came about by mistake, and fragments of the Gospel of Mary which contains supposedly secret saying that Jesus revealed to Mary Magdalene. The badly damaged

Below: *Triad (trinity) of the Aten, Akhenaten and Nefertiti showing blessings being dispensed upon the King and Queen with hands holding Ankh's towards them*

Facing page: *The Bust of Nefertiti who was the chief wife of Akhenaten. This was discovered in a sculptor's shop in the city of Akhetaten (Tel-el Amarna). Nefertiti has been hailed as one of the most beautiful and fascinating women of all time*

Gospel of Judas was discovered in 1978, though not published until 2006. It makes out Judas to be a hero and it was dismissed by the church Father Irenaeus in AD180 as 'fictitious history'. These books were all written too late to be considered alongside the four Gospels and were immediately rejected by the churches. Contrary to what some imagine, none of the Gnostic writings claim that Jesus married Mary Magdalene—nor do any other documents of the first four centuries.

Oxyrhynchus, city of the Sharp-nosed fish

Here the Oxyrhynchus (sharp-nosed) fish was worshipped.

Above: *Many papyrus documents have survived well in the hot Egyptian sand. Like this one of an Oxyrhynchus papyrus with Euclid's Elements*

Excavations by Grenfell and Hunt yielded vast quantities of Greek, Coptic and Arabic papyri, which are slowly being studied and published. Many of them reveal how normal life was, a letter from Theon to his father said, 'If you do not send for me I won't eat, I won't drink so there'! One of the earliest discoveries was part of the apocryphal *Gospel of Thomas* a collection of 114 supposed sayings of Jesus.

Above: *The figures depicted in this tomb at Beni Hasan are from Palestine in the time of the patriarchs*

Beni Hasan

These ancient tombs contain fascinating wall paintings that depict many areas of life. The tomb of Khnumhotep (No 3) has one of thirty-seven people from Palestine entering Egypt to sell eye paint. They were painted in the time of the Patriarchs (2050–1786 BC) and show how Abraham, Jacob and Joseph and their families may have looked.

Above: *A boundary stela at Akhetaten (Tel El-Amarna,) Akhenaten's new city to the god Aten*

Below: *A small statue of Akhenaten wearing the blue crown. He was considered to be the heretic Pharaoh*

Akhenaten (Amenhotep IV)

This king has had more written about him than any other including Tutankhamun. His strange physique and devotion to the Aten has led many to call him the forerunner of Moses and of Jesus Christ. The early date for the Exodus favoured in this book means that Akhenaten was a follower and not a precursor of Moses. Akhenaten's reign was later to be described as an illness on the land, because during his time in power he redirected worship. The enormity of Akhenaten's challenge to Egyptian traditions was shown

Above: *The pathway to the Northern Tombs at Amarna*

in that he shook the priesthood to its foundations and struck at the very heart of Egyptian religion. Akhenaten not only removed the conventional gods, but he changed his name from Amenhotep to reflect his worship of the god Aten (Akhenaten means 'worshipper of Aten'), and revealed a new trinity comprising the Aten, Akhenaten and his queen Nefertiti. For all this, he was considered a heretic.

After his death, the young Tutankhamun reinstated the traditional worship of Egypt and Akhenaten's temples, monuments and images were destroyed and expunged from the records. Akhenaten had gone against all things that were considered to be normal and therefore this heretic must be consigned to the rubbish heap of history—until the diligent archaeologists brought him back to life.

Below: *Royal correspondence is contained on the Armana clay tablets*

Tel El-Amarna (Akhetaten)

This is the site of Akhetaten, 'The horizon of the Aten', Akhenaten's new city on the banks of the Nile started in his fifth year. It is, best known today as Tell El-Amarna, a name coined in the nineteenth century. All buildings and life were dedicated to the Aten, the living Sun-disk, described as 'he who decrees life, the lord of sunbeams, maker of brightness; he causes everyone to live and people are never sated with seeing him.' Amarna was over 15km (9 mi) north to south and contained magnificent temples and palaces, although many of them have been destroyed. Nevertheless, recent and ongoing archaeological work has revealed enough to give a glimpse of this long dead city.

***Above:** A colossal statue of Akhenaten revealing his peculiar appearance that has led to a number of theories that he may have suffered from a genetic disease*

Amarna letters

The Amarna letters are part of a collection of 382 tablets that were discovered from 1887 at El-Amarna in Egypt. They throw interesting light on the political situation in the 14th century BC when Egyptian power was beginning to decline. Akkadian in cuneiform script (*cuneatus* being Latin for wedge-shaped) had become the lingua franca for international communications and was the language used on the Amarna letters. These letters from various subject rulers in Canaan to Amenhotep III and Amenhotep IV (Akhenaten) include increasingly desperate pleas for assistance against the growing strength of homeless groups. Some name the *Hapiru* (or *Habiru*), which, if we accept the fifteenth century date for the Exodus, may be an early reference to the Hebrew invaders. The appeal for help against these people would fit well the period of conquest under Joshua and the Judges. Letter EA 290 refers to 'a town belonging to Jerusalem, *Bit-Nin Urta*'—probably Bethlehem.

***Above:** Osireion at Abydos where Osiris was supposed to be buried*

The Plagues on Egypt—God versus the gods

The character of the plagues challenged so many of Egypt's gods, and their failure to intervene would have been seen as a terrible judgement on them. Maat, the goddess of order, harmony and stability was helpless, along with the king, and his magicians who would have invoked Isis, the goddess of immense magical powers (Exodus 9:11).

Some of the gods challenged by the plagues

1. The waters turned to blood.

Khnum, the ram god, creator of life the guardian of the Nile sources.

Hapi, god of the Nile and spirit of the Nile.

Osiris, the god of the underworld whose bloodstream was the Nile.

Sobek, the crocodile god, called the god of water.

2. Frogs

Hekat, goddess of fertility and childbirth.

3. Gnats

The priests commonly threw dust on their heads to symbolize contrition and humility.

4. Flies.

Horus, the falcon god of the air, which was now inundated with flies.

Khepre r, symbolized as the flying beetle.

5. Livestock.

Apis, Buchis, Mnevis, the bull gods.

Hathor, Heset, Mehet-Weret Shentayat, the cow goddesses.

Amun, Kherty, Khnum, the ram gods.

6. Boils.

Imhotep, the Healer.

Sekhmet, the goddess of creating epidemics and bringing them to an end.

7. Hail. Nut, the sky goddess.

Osiris, a god intimately connected to grain.

8. Locusts.

Min, the god of fertility.

Geb, the earth god who provides the nourishment and fruits of the earth.

9. Darkness.

Ra, in his many manifestations considered the supreme deity.

Shu, the god of sunlight and air.

10. The death of the firstborn.

Heir, represented special qualities of life and strength especially for the royal succession, so this was a great blow against Pharaoh, the son of Ra on Earth.

***Above:** The Temple at Abydos was a sacred site in Ancient Egypt*

Abydos

This was one of the most sacred sites in ancient Egypt, because it was the cult centre for Osiris, god of the dead. All ancient Egyptians tried to come here at least once in their lifetime or they hoped to be buried here. In New Kingdom tombs, the inscriptions often showed the deceased making a symbolic pilgrimage to Abydos to become associated with Osiris. According to Egyptian mythology, Horus' wicked brother Seth had murdered Osiris, and his body was disposed of in the Nile before ending up in the Mediterranean Sea. Isis, Osiris' sister and consort, decided to retrieve his body, and after many set backs was able to use her magic to bury his dismembered remains. Meanwhile Osiris had taken up the position of king of the dead in the *Duat*, the Egyptian underworld. The Osireion behind Seti's temple is said to be the burial place of Osiris. Egyptians

Above: *Beautiful coloured wall sculpture of the god Anubis and Seti I in the Temple at Abydos*

Below: *Uncoloured wall sculpture at Abydos of Seti I offering incense to an enthroned Horus*

Above: *King list of Seti I and a young Ramesses II at Abydos*

Below: *At Abydos Ramesses II lassoing a bull with his approving father Seti I behind him*

venerated the health-granting Eye of Horus, or wedjet; this represented the eye restored to Horus after he lost it avenging the murder of his father, Osiris.

The great temples of Seti I and Ramesses II are well worth visiting. Seti's temple is dedicated not only to Osiris, his wife Isis and son Horus, but also to the national gods, Amun-Ra, Ptah, Re-Horakhty and the dead king himself. The temples were constructed using white limestone, and are beautifully decorated with raised painted reliefs that are possibly the finest in Egypt. A temple dedicated to Sesostris III (possibily pharaoh at the time of Joseph) is at South Abydos.

Dendera

Here the goddess Hathor supposedly gave birth to the god Ihy, the child of Horus. Hathor who was worshipped in many forms, is represented in her most universal role, that of a lovely young woman, patroness of joy, music, and the dance. The sistrum, a rattle like instrument considered sacred to Hathor, was used in temple rituals to purify the gods and ward off evil (see 2 Samuel 6:5).

This temple was buried under the sands until the 19th century and so has been remarkably preserved. The monumental gateway dates from the reign of the Roman Emperor Domitian who may have exiled John to Patmos (Revelation 1:9). To the right beyond the gate, are a Roman Mammisi (birth house), and a late fifth century AD Coptic church; this is an excellent example of an early Egyptian church. The vestibule of the main temple contains inscriptions from many emperors, some of whom are referred to in the Bible, Augustus (Luke 2:1), Tiberius (Matthew 22:19), Caligula (not in the Bible), Claudius (Acts 18:2) and Nero (Philippians 4:22). The Hypostyle Hall with its various compartments is splendid, and a trip into the subterranean crypts which were probably used for storage, reveals vibrant paintings. A walk to the roof up a dark staircase with ten right-angled bends is rewarded when, surprisingly, the Temple roof is revealed to be on several levels and offers glorious views of the whole site. There are a number of chambers, and in the second one

Below: *The Temple at Dendera is a wonderful site to visit because of the extent and completeness of the temple complex*

Above: *Details of the ceiling in the Temple at Dendera showing the star constellations sailing across the sky in boats*

Left: On the back wall of the Temple at Dendera you can see a representation of Cleopatra (VII) and her son, Cesarion

is a cast of the famous 'Zodiac of Dendera'. This is the only circular representation of the heavens found in Egypt. The original has been in the Louvre Paris since 1922.

On New Year's day Hathor's statue was carried up the west staircase to the open-air kiosk on the roof where it was revitalised by the sun. Hathor was the goddess of pleasure and love and the lover of Horus. Each year her statue was taken on a sacred barque to Edfu where the Festival of Drunkenness celebrated their divine union.

The south rear wall of the temple has colossal carved figures of the famous Queen Cleopatra VII and her son by Julius Caesar, Caesarion, making offerings to the gods. If time permits, a walk around the walls of the temple reveals many reliefs and inscriptions of the emperors, predominantly Nero. To the south of the Temple lies the smaller Temple to Isis built in the reign of Augustus (Luke 2:1).

Below: *View from the roof of the main temple at Dendera showing the boundary of the complex*

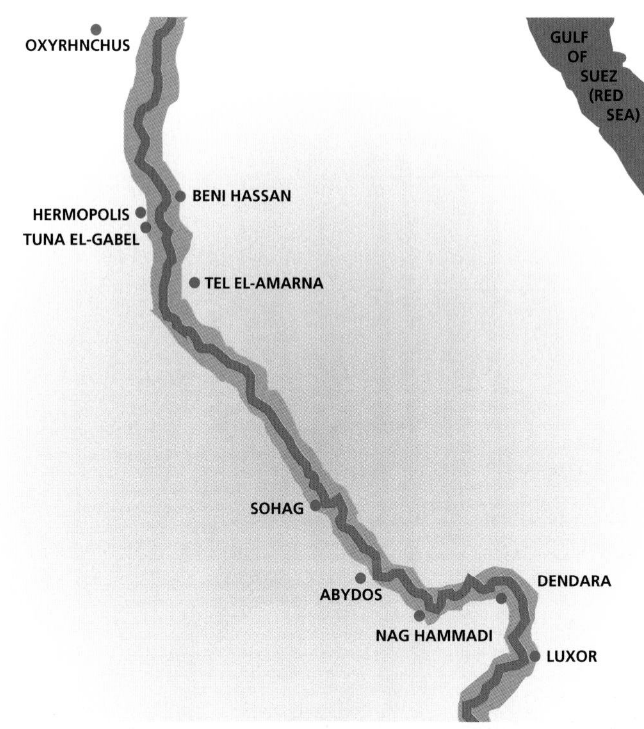

SHOWING THE LOCATION OF THE SITES MENTIONED IN THIS CHAPTER

TRAVEL INFORMATION

Beni Hasan

The rock tombs are on the edge of the desert and are 271km (168mi) south of Cairo and 35km (22mi) north of Armana.

Tel El-Amarna (Akhetaten)

Situated 306km (190mi) south of Cairo. It can be visited by rail; the station is 11km (7mi) from Dier Mawas, or by car, but is best appreciated from the River Nile. If not part of an organised tour then you can hire a donkey to get around this vast site. Unless especially interested in the Amarna period, it is best to focus on the main city rather then venture out to see the many tombs; the northern ones are 5km (3mi) to the east and the Royal tomb the same distance beyond them. If visiting the tombs it is advisable to carry a torch.

Abydos

This important ancient site is 524km (325mi) from Cairo and 150km (95mi) NW of Luxor.

Nag Hammadi

These scant ruins are located 556km (345mi) from Cairo, and many tourists do not bother to visit this place.

Dendera

The temple is well worth exploring. It is opposite the town of Qena, 612km (380mi) south of Cairo and 62km (38.5mi) N of Luxor.

6 Terror, temples and ancient texts

Thebes (modern Luxor) stood on both sides of the Nile and was the 'Thebes of the Greeks', celebrated for its hundred gates by Homer in his Iliad. In grandeur and extent it can only be compared to Nineveh and Babylon

Thebes was the ancient capital of Upper Egypt, mentioned in the Bible only in Jeremiah 46:25, Ezekiel 30:14–16, and Nahum 3:8. Thebes was first captured by the Assyrians in the time of Sargon II (Isaiah 20:1), then by Ashurbanipal (Ezra 4:10) before being delivered into the hand of the Babylonian Nebuchadnezzar II (Jeremiah 46:24–26).

Terror from the North

Ashurbanipal, the last great king of Assyria, succeeded to the throne when his father, Esarhaddon (2 Kings 19:37; Ezra 4:2), died on his way to campaign in Egypt in 669 BC. Esarhaddon's death caused the Pharaoh Taharqa, whom Sennacherib's spokesman had thirty-two years earlier called, 'that splintered reed of a staff which pierces a man's hand and wounds him if he leans on it!' (Isaiah 36:6), to launch an offensive against the Assyrian garrison stationed at Memphis in 667 BC. Ashurbanipal despatched his rapid response units and retook the lost territory. In the Pergamum museum in Berlin is a large stone stela of Esarhaddon with the much smaller figures of Baalu king of Tyre and Pharaoh Taharqa cowering in fear before him. When Taharqa's nephew Tantamnni became Pharaoh, he tried to regain control of Memphis and the Delta region. In response, Ashurbanipal reacted with another invasion, but this time he did not stop and pushed down the Nile to Thebes. The fall of Thebes in 664 BC is a key date for the history of the ancient world in general and the Old Testament in particular and is attested by a number of sources.

Above: *Pylon Entrance to the Great Temple of Karnak*

Facing page: *The Statue of Ramesses II in Karnak Temple proclaims his might and power*

***Left:** Karnak Temple was the largest place of worship in the ancient world*

Egypt was no match for the might of the Assyrian army: the city capitulated, its treasures were looted and many of its people were deported. Ashurbanipal left the Egyptians Necho and his son Psamtik in charge of Egypt, and when they asserted their independence in 656 BC Ashurbanipal did not return. Cambyses, king of the Persians (525 BC), laid Thebes waste by fire, and it was ruined by Ptolemy Lathyrus in 81BC.

Joseph in prison

In Egypt, prisons (commonly called the *Khenret,* 'place of confinement') did exist, but imprisonment was both costly and non-productive, and was generally used only to hold those awaiting trial. Convicted criminals might be exiled to a work-gang or given a physical punishment ranging from beating and wounding through mutilation of the face to death by impaling on a post. When Joseph was falsely accused after resisting the feminine charms of Potiphar's wife, he ended up in prison (Genesis 39:20) probably in Thebes, away from the centre of court at Memphis in the North. The head of state bureaucracy the vizier–ironically Joseph himself would eventually hold this position–could decree that the offender be held in the foreboding

***Right:** An avenue of Rams representing the god Amun linked the Temples of Karnak and Luxor*

sounding Great Prison. The Great Prison at Thebes was one of a series of prisons and small jails dotted all over Egypt, and it was an institution that fulfilled several functions:

It was the repository of criminal records (might Joseph's be found one day?), and therefore it served as the legal archive.

It housed the law-court and cells.

It was the place where punishment was swiftly carried out.

It could also serve as a barrack or work house.

Temple worship and ritual

There were two main types of temple: cult temples for deities and mortuary temples for kings, but all were designed to a regular pattern. A typical layout would have begun with a processional way leading to a main gateway known as a Pylon (see Glossary page 113). Inside was the peristyle court, a large open space surrounded by a colonnade. This led into the hypostyle (meaning 'under pillars') hall with a roof supported by columns, which then led to the inner sanctum containing the god's shrine. The floor of the temples represented the earth, the columns took the forms of plants rising from the earth, and the ceilings were the sky, often decorated with stars or astronomical representations.

Access to Egypt's temples was restricted to the priesthood, the servants of the gods, with only the king, as Egypt's supreme high priest and sole intermediary between people and the gods, entering the inner sanctuary to address the image of the god directly. This small chamber was considered to be the holiest place, and was located in the darkest and most remote part of the temple. The cult statue of the god must have been impressive, made of gold and silver, inlaid with precious stones including lapis lazuli and turquoise. Each of these would have held symbolic value: gold was the flesh of the gods, silver their bones, and lapis lazuli their hair. By contrast the Israelites were expressly forbidden to create anything that resembled their God (Exodus 20:4–6), although it did not take them long to disobey this commandment (Exodus 32:1–4).

Above: *An unfinished column at Karnak Temple*

***Right:** Behind the Pylon at Karnak Temple are the remains of the mud brick retaining wall that was to have been removed when the Pylon was completed. Compare Exodus 5:7*

In Israel only one temple was required as a symbol of the people's unity in the worship of the one true God.

At dawn, the purified priests would form a solemn procession and approach the inner sanctuary in clouds of purifying incense. Upon entering the sanctuary the high priest declared: 'It is the king who sends me to see the god.' He would then break the clay seals on the doors of the shrine to reveal the god's statue, upon which he used the words of a hymn to awaken the divine spirit in the statue. He then announced: 'I have seen the god and the powerful one has seen me' before kissing the ground before the statue. Various rituals were carried out before the first offerings of the day, including (at Karnak) vast quantities of bread, meat, fowl, fruit, vegetables, honey, milk, wine, beer, water, perfumes, oils, incense, salt, natron clothing, jewellery, lamps and all manner of regalia. The general population gave food and drink as a form of taxation, but the king made donations in proportion to the current prosperity of the country. Millions of flowers were also used, as the perfume of flowers was regard as the essence of the gods. Once the god had enjoyed his fill of these things, a ritual called 'Reversion of Offerings' was performed in which the priests took away all the food and drink for their own consumption; unsurprisingly many grew fat on what was offered!

Temple of Karnak

After a century of foreign occupation, the New Kingdom of Egypt emerged (1550–1150 BC) with its capital at Thebes. Karnak and Luxor temples together were known as *Waset*. Thebes was the later Greek name for the town and was embellished with grandiose temples worthy of the majesty of the pharaohs. The temple of Karnak is the biggest temple complex in the world, covering an area of 100 hectares and known as *Ipet-isut* ('most select of places') by the ancient Egyptians. In the eighteenth dynasty it was called the Heliopolis of the South.

Karnak is a city of temples built by thirty Pharaohs taking over 2000 years to construct with twenty-five temples and

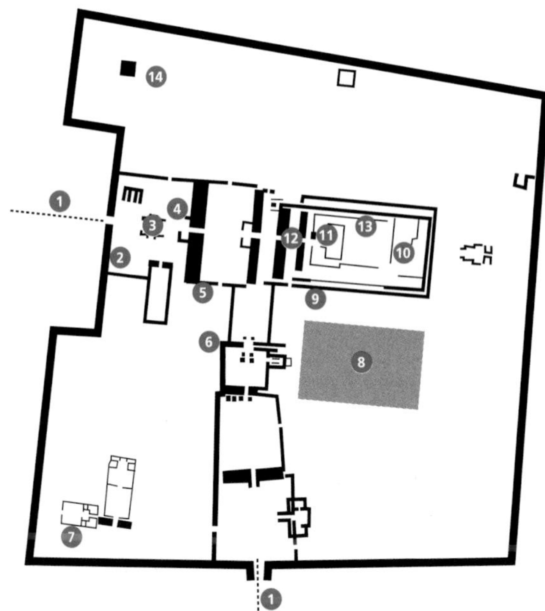

SHOWING THE LAYOUT OF THE CENTRAL ENCLOSURE OF KARNAK TEMPLE

1 AVENUES OF SPHINXES
2 REMAINS OF MUD RAMP BEHIND PYLON
3 KIOSK OF TAHARQA
4 COLOSSUS OF RAMESSES II
5 SHISHAK'S INSCRIPTIONS
6 SEVENTH PYLON
7 OPET TEMPLE
8 SACRED LAKE
9 CAFE
10 FESTIVAL HALL OF TUTMOSIS III
11 SIXTH PYLON
12 OBELISK OF HATSHEPSUT
13 TUTMOSIS III CANAANITE CITY LIST
14 OPEN AIR MUSEUM

***Left:** Shishak's City List reveals his campaigns in Israel—see 1 Kings 14:25–26*

chapels in the complex dedicated to the Theben triad of Amun, Mut and Khonsu. Each of them had a precinct in the temple complex, the greatest and largest belonging to Amun. There was also a precinct for Montu, the falcon-headed local god. There is so much to see at Karnak, including the imposing Pylon (a monumental gateway) that is 130m (426.5ft) long by 43m (141ft) high and 10m (33ft) deep, with recesses for flags. The first court contains the only surviving massive papyrus-shaped column of Taharqa and the colossi of Ramesses II which was usurped by Pinudjem in the 21st Dynasty.

Shishak's City List

On the south end of the Second Pylon, is the Triumphal Inscription of Sheshonq I (945–924 BC), the Shishak of 1 Kings 14:25–26 who invaded Israel and Judah in 925 BC and carried off the treasures of Jerusalem's temple. It celebrates the King's victory over Rehoboam of Judah, the son of Solomon. To the left is a large figure of Amun holding in his right hand the curved sword of victory and in his left hand cords binding five rows of captured cities, each represented by a circuit of walls bearing its name and the upper part of the body of a fettered prisoner. The hooked noses, prominent cheekbones and beards identify the prisoners as Semitic. The Bible records the attack from Judah's perspective (1 Kings 14:25–26 and 2 Chronicles 12:2–4, 9), but Shishak's list gives much greater detail including the names of 150 cities. Only a few of the cities mentioned in the reliefs can be identified with certainty; these include Rabbath (last in the first row), Taanach, Shunem, Rehob, Haphraim, Mahanaim, Gibeon, Beth-Horon, Kedemoth, Ajalon, Megiddo, and Arad (in second row), the rest cannot be located today. Next to these are the reliefs of Ramesses II showing his military exploits in Palestine and Syria, including the famous Battle of Kadesh.

Ramesses' Treaty

Here also is Ramesses II's accord with the Hittites which is known as the first peace treaty in history. Originally written on silver tablets in Heliopolis and Hattusus, a copy was found here on this wall in the Karnak Temple. After years of inconclusive battles between the Hittites and the Egyptians, Ramesses II and the Hittite ruler concluded an agreement by which Syria and Canaan would be divided between them. On either side of this text are depictions of

Above: *Taharqa's column at Karnak*

Right: Tourists see how many it takes to encircle one of Karnak's mighty columns

Below: Thutmosis III Canaanite City List is a valuable tool in understanding the timeline of ancient history

Merneptah's battles in Canaan, including those against Ashkelon and Israel.

The Second Pylon opens into the Great Hypostyle Hall—a most impressive place. Here there are 134 papyrus columns, the centre twelve are 21m (69ft) tall, and the remaining 122 columns are 15m (49ft) tall. A guide will sometimes point out where a murder in the film of Agatha Christie's *Death on the Nile* was almost committed.

Thutmosis' Canaanite City List

The Sixth Pylon contains Tuthmosis III's City Lists. Here, hundreds of princes are shown with hands tied behind their backs and with cartouches on their shields. This is a depiction of the rulers of the cities of Canaan that Tuthmosis III captured when Megiddo fell. All the rulers, except the king of Kadesh, were trapped in Megiddo, and so by the capture of Megiddo Tuthmosis could say that it was as the capture of a thousand cities. At Tuthmosis' death the Egyptian empire stretched from the Euphrates to the Fourth Cataract the greatest ever extent of Egypt's territory. When Germanicus, the nephew of the Roman emperor Tiberius (Luke 3:1), visited Karnak in AD 19 he asked one of the priests to explain to him the long list of Tuthmosis III's military exploits depicted on the walls.

Behind this is the Festival Temple of Tuthmosis III, anciently called Most Splendid of Monuments and built as a memorial temple to Tuthmosis and his ancestral cult. The pillars inside the hall are said to imitate the ancient tent poles of a pavilion, unique in Egyptian architecture; they still clearly show the coloured decoration. A king list here omits the female Pharaoh Hatshepsut his predecessor because she was perceived to have gone against tradition and Maat, therefore upsetting Egypt's normal order (see page 10).

Can you hear me?

In the area leading towards Karnak's east gate, Ramesses II built a small Temple of the Hearing Ear, where local inhabitants of Thebes would bring their requests for the priests to petition the gods of Karnak.

To the south of the Temple of Amun is the Sacred Lake. The area in the foreground was originally a fowl yard, and the domesticated birds belonging to Amun were driven from here through a stone tunnel into the lake each day. Seating overlooks the lake for the modern Sound and Light show, and underneath here the remains of priests' houses have been found.

The Roman emperor, Constantine the Great, embraced Christianity in the 4th century AD and issued orders for the closure of pagan temples in the Roman Empire. The Romans built a Christian chapel in the ruins of Karnak temple and drew pictures of saints and wrote Coptic inscriptions on the walls of the Festival Hall of Thutmose III.

When the pharaoh Akhenaten (Amenhoteph IV) abandoned the traditional worship of Amun and took up the worship of Aten, the sun god (see page 65), he built a huge temple to Aten at Karnak to the East of the one for Amun, and called it the *Gempaaten*. After his death, the priests at Thebes destroyed all signs of sun worship, including the temple that defiled Karnak. The size and scope of this amazing structure is slowly coming to light.

An avenue of ram-headed sphinxes, sacred to Amun, now partially destroyed or buried, once connected the great Temple of Karnak to the Temple of Luxor (see picture on page 76). It marked the route taken at the festival of Opet when the sacred statues of

Left: *Priests bathed in Karnak's sacred Temple Lake*

Priests of Egypt

Priests were referred to as *hem netjer*, 'servant of the god'. The King was considered to be the sole earthly intermediary between the gods and the people. In practice he needed to delegate this duty to the High Priest of each deity. By the eighteenth dynasty, Amun was the most powerful of the gods and the high priest bore the title, 'first prophet of Amun'. During the plagues on Egypt Aaron became the first prophet of YHWH to Pharaoh, and Moses appeared as God to him (Exodus 4:16).

At Karnak, the god Amun was served by a vast number of ritually pure priests (81,000 during the reign of Ramesses III). They removed all body hair and bathed four times a day in the sacred Temple Lake before wearing untainted linen robes to signify their purity. The Hebrews would have learnt a lot about ritual purity in Egypt and the inference should have been drawn: if these men take so much trouble in the worship of idols how much more care should be taken in the worship of the one true God. (Exodus 19:6. See also 1 Peter 1:22 and 2:5).

Lector priests (*hery heb*) were responsible for reading out the rituals from the sacred texts. *Hour* priests, who were astronomers, were responsible for studying the stars in order to determine the correct times for rituals and festivals. Another official, with the title 'bearer of floral offerings', prepared flowers used in worship. The ritual performance of music and dance was provided by high born women who were referred to as: 'chief of the entertainers'.

the gods, Amun, Mut and Khonsu were taken out on procession to Luxor Temple. When the celebrations were complete the Pharaoh escorted them back to Karnak on the Nile.

Luxor Temple

In ancient Egypt the temple area now known as Luxor was called *Ipt rsyt*, the 'Southern Sanctuary', referring to the holy of holies at the temple's southern end, in which the principal god Amun, dwelt 'pre-eminent in his sanctuary'. Two red granite obelisks originally stood in front of the first pylon at the rear of the forecourt but only one, more than 25m (82ft) high, now remains. The other was removed to Paris where it now stands in the centre of the Place de la Concorde. Luxor derives from the Arabic *al-uksur*,

Above: *Hatshepsut's mighty obelisk towers over all at Karnak*

meaning fortifications. That name in addition, was adapted from the Latin *castrum* which referred to the Roman fort built around the temple in the later third century AD. The temple of Luxor, since its inception, has always been considered a sacred site, and it was the power base of the living and the foremost national shrine of King Amenhotep III, who reigned 1390–1353 BC. He built this beautiful temple and dedicated it to Amun-Ra, king of the gods, his consort Mut, and their son Khons. It has been in almost continuous use as a place of worship right up to the present day (see below). It was completed by Tutankhamun and Horemheb and added to by Ramesses II. Towards the rear is a granite shrine dedicated to Alexander the Great where the king is depicted with a ram's horn crown (Daniel 8:5).

The Roman emperor Diocletian (AD 284–305) crushed all rebellion in Egypt and transformed the entire Temple of Luxor into a legionary fortress centred on the worship of the divine emperor—himself! Diocletian's persecution of Christians was so vicious that his reign still inaugurates the

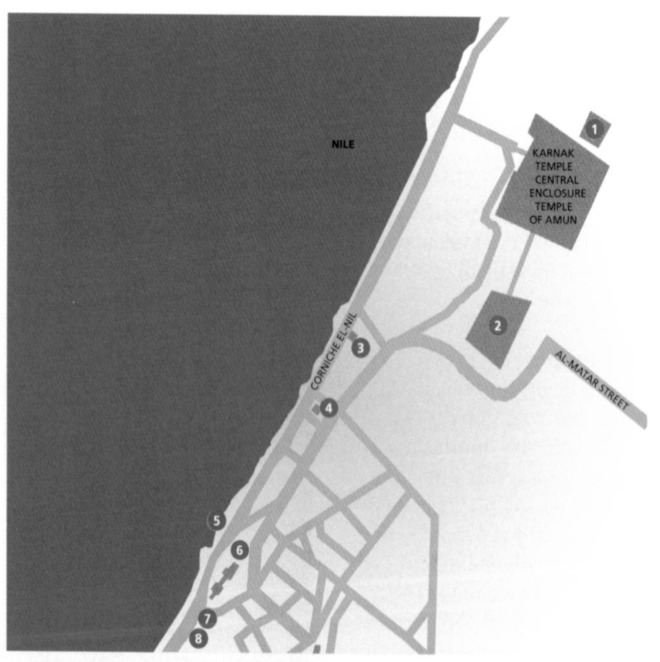

THE MAJOR SITES OF LUXOR

1 NORTHERN ENCLOSURE - TEMPLE OF MONTU
2 SOUTHERN ENCLOSURE - TEMPLE OF MUT
3 CHICAGO HOUSE
4 LUXOR MUSEUM
5 MUSEUM OF MUMMIFICATION
6 LUXOR TEMPLE
7 TOURIST BAZAAR (ABUDUI'S BOOKSHOP)
8 WINTER PALACE HOTEL

Left: Mosque Abul Haggag built on the buried ruins of Luxor Temple now sits perched high on the structure of the first court of Ramesses II

Era of Martyrs in the calendar of the Coptic Church. Less then fifty years later, the emperor Constantine reversed Diocletian's actions when he embraced Christianity.

Late classical Roman paintings overlaid the Egyptian reliefs of Amenhotep III, and during the Christian era the temple's Hypostyle Hall was converted into a Christian church, and the remains of another Coptic church can be seen to the west. Then, for thousands of years the temple was buried beneath the streets and houses of the town of Luxor. Eventually the mosque of Abul Haggag was built over it. This mosque was preserved when the temple was uncovered, and it forms an integral part of the site today with its entrance on the east side and on the west a drop of a few metres rendering the old doorway inaccessible.

An ancient text of the New Testament

To the locals and visitors who sit on the veranda of the Old Palace Hotel in Luxor sipping tea in the suffocating heat of a summer afternoon, a commemorative brass plaque at the entrance may seem no more than another attractive hieroglyph. It reads: 'In loving memory of the Rev Charles Bousfield Huleatt M.A. chaplain at Luxor 1893–1901: who perished in the earthquake at his post of duty as chaplain at Messina in 1908. Well done good and faithful servant, enter thou into the joy of thy Lord. Matt. xxv.2l.'

This Hotel, with its modest Anglican chapel, was probably the finest achievement of the Christian travel entrepreneur Thomas Cook, and it was the setting of Charles Huleatt's life and missionary work. Huleatt unknowingly discovered one of the oldest extant fragments of a New Testament text.

Right: The closed entrance to the Mosque at the Luxor Temple from the temple floor

Charles Bousfield Huleatt and the Magdalen fragment

After ordination in Hereford Cathedral, Huleatt spent the winter of 1890–91 as English chaplain at Luxor, a post he was to take up every winter from 1893–1901. The climate suited Huleatt's frail health and the contact with well-informed travellers from many walks of life was intellectually stimulating. During his time in Egypt Huleatt acquired three scraps of papyrus which he considered very important and arranged to have them sent by recorded post to his old Oxford college, Magdalen, in October 1901. There they lay largely forgotten until on Christmas Eve 1994 Huleatt's fragments leapt into the limelight when *The Times* reported an extraordinary claim made by the German papyrologist, Carsten Peter Thiede that 'A papyrus believed to be the oldest extant fragment of the New Testament has been found in an Oxford library … It provides the first material evidence that the Gospel according to St Matthew is an eyewitness account written by the contemporaries of Christ.'

Not since the discovery of the Dead Sea Scrolls in 1947 had there been such an important, albeit controversial, announcement. What Huleatt had sent to Oxford in 1901, shortly before his tragic death in an earthquake, was ten verses from Matthew 28 that had formed part of a codex (a book as opposed to a scroll). The identification is virtually undisputed but whilst Thiede and others, with strong reasons, concluded the text was written before AD 70, some scholars, unwilling for such an early date, suggest late in the second century.

Right: *Old Winter Palace Hotel where Howard Carter announced the discovery of Tutankhamun's tomb. Here also is the plaque to Huleatt*

TRAVEL INFORMATION

Luxor

Luxor is 676km (420mi) South of Cairo, and 223km (138.5mi) north of Aswan.

The airport is 7km (4.3mi) east of the town.

Luxor Temple
Shari El-Bahr El-Nil

Near to the Old Winter Palace Hotel

The site is very close to the Nile and looks delightful, when illuminated at night.

Old Winter Palace Hotel
Now called, Sofitel Winter Palace Luxor
Corniche el Nile
Street 0 Luxor, Egypt
☎ (+20)95/2380425 — (+20)95/2374087
H1661@sofitel.com

Lord Carnarvon and Howard Carter announced in this hotel that they had discovered Tutankhamun's tomb in the Valley of the Kings

Luxor Museum
Located on the Corniche halfway between Luxor and Karnak Temples.

This is a superb museum and very well laid out. The Museum includes items from Tutankhamun's tomb, wall panels from Akhenaten's temple, a statue of a painfully restrained criminal, and the mummies of

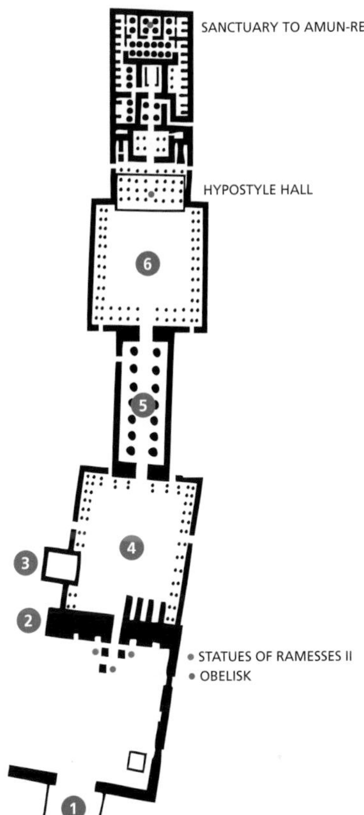

THE LAYOUT OF LUXOR TEMPLE

Ramesses I and Ahmose; perhaps the pharaoh who ordered the death of the Hebrew boys (Exodus 1:16).

Unfortunately the Museum does not appear to have a website, but there are various sites that well describe the Museum and what it offers.

Karnak Temple

The Karnak Temple is huge covering a site almost 500 hectares (2 sq. mi), and is located about 2.5km (1.5 mi) north of Luxor. An excellent Son et Lumiere, is held here each evening, check locally for timings and languages being used.

Luxor Tourist Office, Nile Street, Luxor ☎ (095) 382 215 or 373 294

Transport: Buses run from the Luxor Bus station, taxis can be hired, or go by horse drawn caleche. Most visit as part of an organised tour.

Below: *Statue of Ramesses II flanks the entrance to the Pylon at Luxor temple*

7 The curse of the mummy

'They who enter this sacred tomb shall swift be visited by wings of death'—the supposed inscription from Tutankhamun's tomb invented by journalists after the death of Lord Carnarvon in Cairo

Why let truth get in the way of a good story? That is the angle taken on the so-called mummy's curse, yet death was surprisingly long in coming for those who were closest to the work. The main candidate for the curse, Howard Carter, discovered and entered the tomb in 1922, but he did not die until 1939 at the age of 64. Dr Douglas E. Derry who performed the autopsy on Tutankhamun was 87 when he died in 1969, and Lady Evelyn Herbert, who was one of the first to enter the tomb, was 79 when she died in 1980.

Valley of the Kings

(A full list of known tombs is on page 119). Located here is possibly the most famous set of graves in the world. Pharaohs of the New Kingdom c. 1567–1085BC decided to be buried in this remote place as it was less conspicuous than pyramids and cheaper to create an eternal dwelling place with concealed entrances. Unfortunately many of them have been ransacked, possibly by those who constructed them.

The tomb of Tuthmosis III is accessed up a long staircase, but is a superb one to visit. In the burial chamber are wonderful depictions of Tuthmosis entering the afterlife. One inscription, 'the Tenth Hour', shows a large block of water called Deep Waters and High Banks, and contains the bodies of those who died without proper burial. Could this be a reference to the Exodus (Exodus 14:27)?

The tomb of Amenhotep II has over 90 steps down to the burial chamber, where his mummified body was found. A cache of mummies was found in a side

Above: *Princess Diana's Factory for Alabaster near the Valley of the Kings*

Facing page: *Arial view of a west bank village showing ancient paths leading to the Valley of the Kings*

Howard Carter

The English Egyptologist, Howard Carter, was born in London, on 9 May 1874. He was the son of Samuel John Carter an animal painter. From an early age Howard showed an aptitude for drawing and this, coupled with his interest in Egyptian antiquities, encouraged him to travel to Egypt at the age of 17. There he served for eight years with the Egyptian Exploration Fund, working with Flinders Petrie (see page 41) at Amarna and as a member of the team making an epigraphic recording of the Temple of Hatshepsut at Deir el-Bahri.

In 1900 Carter was appointed Chief Inspector of Antiquities to the Egyptian Government Antiquities Organisation with responsibilities for Upper Egypt. He stayed in this post until late in 1904 when he was moved to the post of Chief Inspector for Lower Egypt.

With the Earl of Carnarvon funding the dig in the Valley of the Kings, Carter discovered the first steps leading to the tomb of Tutankhamun on 4 November 1922. He immediately sent a telegram to Carnarvon in England, who arrived by 26 November and watched as Carter made a hole in the door of the tomb. Holding a candle, Carter leaned in to take a look. Behind him Lord Carnarvon asked, 'Can you see anything?' Carter answered, 'Yes, wonderful things.' Work on the clearance and recording of the contents of the tomb continued until the concession ran out in 1929. Failing health and other commitments meant that Carter never published a detailed scholarly account of the tomb. Howard Carter died 2 March 1939, in Kensington London and was buried in Putney Vale Cemetery, South West London.

room near here including those of Tuthmosis IV, Amenhotep III and Merneptah. The tombs of Horemheb and Merneptah are deep and hot but the visit is worthwhile.

Tutankhamun's tomb is the most famous but very small and it is located in the centre of the Valley.

The magnificent tomb of Seti I, discovered by the Italian adventurer Belzoni, is almost as long as St Paul's cathedral in London!

KV5 is the tomb of the sons of Ramesses II and was considered to be insignificant. It has now be shown to be the largest yet discovered in the Valley, with over 100 rooms that are still being excavated.

Moses would undoubtedly have been familiar with this place and may have attended more then one burial here.

When the human remains of these famous kings were transported to Cairo, an ancient scene was re-enacted. Without any urging or coercing, women lined the route to the River Nile bewailing the passing of these bodies on what was now to become a final journey. Less glamorously, the train company wanted the dockets attached to each mummy to have a suitable description of the cargo to be transported. Someone wrote on the dockets, 'dried fish!' Have any such powerful and wealthy kings been subject to such degradation?

Right: Amenhotep II was discovered lying in his sarcophagus in the Valley of the Kings. His body was taken to Cairo for safe keeping

Below Right: The natural pyramid over the Valley of the Kings where it was believed the coiled serpent goddess Meretseger, 'she who loves silence', dwelt

Valley of the Queens

The French archaeologist, Jean François Champollion, named this place, and although containing eighty tombs, it is not nearly as popular as the Valley of the Kings. The Valley of the Queens contains one of Egypt's greatest treasures, the tomb of Queen Nefertari, chief and favourite wife of Ramesses II. This is regarded as the most beautiful tomb in Egypt and has recently been restored to its former glory. Visitor numbers are strictly controlled to preserve the exquisite decorations.

Tombs of the Nobles

Over 400 tombs of nobles and high officials extend over a large area to the south of the Valley of the Kings. The tomb of Rekhmire (No.100), vizier to Tuthmosis III and Amenhotep II, shows servants at work and taxes and gifts from foreign lands being received. Wall paintings in these tombs offer a valuable insight into the everyday life of the ordinary ancient Egyptian, and therefore of Moses and the Israelites in Egypt.

Colossi of Memnon

Amenhotep III, the grandfather of Tutankhamun, was probably the greatest pharaoh in Egyptian history. He built on a monumental scale and his mortuary temple, which was the largest on the West

The Book of the Dead

There were several versions of the Book of the Dead (sometimes known as the Book of the Two Ways). Gaining access to the happy land, 'located somewhere in the Far West', depended on leading a virtuous life on earth. The deceased had to pass through a series of ordeals: the ferry-man must be persuaded to take the dead across the River of Death, then came the twelve gates guarded by fearful serpents. Amulets and a copy of the Book of the Dead—with relevant spells and a map to work out how to pass the many dangers—were buried with the dead person. At the Lake of Fire, forty-two Assessors read out a list of sins and wrongdoings and the deceased had to swear that he was innocent of them all. If that test was passed, he was admitted to the judgement hall of Osiris, where the heart was weighed against the feather of truth. Sometimes an inscribed scarab beetle has been found placed over the heart of a mummy with the words: 'My heart do not testify against me at the judgement.' If the life had been full of sin, the scales would tip against the deceased and they would be fed to Ammut—the crocodile-headed monster. If the life had been virtuous, the deceased could join the ancestors in the kingdom of the West.

Above: Part of the Book of the Dead from Luxor Museum

Bank, must have been fabulous in its prime as the floor was paved in gold. The colossi of Amenhotep III, flanked by smaller figures of his mother and wife, stood before the temple entrance, they are each carved from a single piece of stone and are 18m (59ft) high. Following an earthquake in 27 BC, they became famous for the sound emitted from the northern statue by the stone warming at sunrise; the Greeks believed that Memnon was greeting his mother Eos (the dawn) and his mother's tears (the dew) fell on her beloved son. This noise ceased following the restoration of the statue by the Emperor Septimus Severus in AD 170.

Ramesseum

Ramesses II ordered the construction of this vast mortuary temple, which took over twenty years to complete, to ensure that he would be remembered for all time. Despite earthquakes and

Above: *One of the Colossi of Memnon standing at the entrance to the demolished mortuary temple of Amenhotep III*

Below: *Among the many tombs in the Valley of the Queens, Nefertari, favourite wife of Rameses II, stands out as a magnificent sepulchre with its exquisite wall paintings.*
©Sylvain Grandadam/Robert Harding

flooding by the river, its imposing ruins are still a wonder to behold. The Hypostyle Hall columns retain their colourful depictions of papyrus and lotus plants symbolising Lower and Upper Egypt. The ruins of innumerable mud brick rooms give an idea of the ones Joseph would have ordered to be constructed (Genesis 41:47–49). At the entrance stood an immense 18m (60ft) high, 1,000 tonne statue of Ramesses II; its ruined head and shoulders now lie in the second court, with other parts scattered over the whole site. This inspired the poem of Percy Bysshe Shelley; published in AD 1818 entitled: Ozymandias.

> I met a traveller from an antique land
> Who said: Two vast and trunkless legs of stone
> Stand in the desert. near them, on the sand,
> Half sunk, a shattered visage lies, whose frown,

Left: *This aerial photo of the Ramesseum reveals the great extent of Ramesses II mortuary temple*

And wrinkled lip, and sneer of cold command,
Tell that its sculptor well those passions read,
Which yet survive, stamped on these lifeless things,
The hand that mocked them, and the heart that fed,
And on the pedestal these words appear:
'My name is Ozymandias, King of Kings:
Look upon my works, ye Mighty, and despair!'
Nothing beside remains. Round the decay
Of that colossal wreck, boundless and bare
The lone and level sands stretch far away.

The great bust of Ramesses II, the younger Memnon, now in the British Museum was found here.

Medinet Habu

The great mortuary temple of Ramesses III, which he called 'The House of a Million Years', is a wonderful example of Egyptian temple construction and the best-preserved mortuary temple. The high gate, modelled on a *migdol* or fortress (Judges 9:50–53), before the First Pylon is the likely location of the assassination attempt against the king (see the Royal Mummy room on pages 57–58). Standing at the entrance to the First Pylon a marvellous perspective is revealed: by a gradual decrease of door size, caused by a lowering of the lintels and a gently sloping floor, the eye is naturally directed to the heart of the Temple where the holy

Above: *Medinet Habu seen from a hot air balloon*

Right: *Medinet Habu's decreasing doorways through to the inner sanctuary*

Below: *Philistines depicted on the Second Pylon at Medinet Habu*

place would have been located. A simple but effective method in teaching people that however astonishing the outward show of religion may appear to be, the centre of attention must be the god. In a far more profound way this was a lesson God's people had to learn, (Deuteronomy 6:4 and Mark 12:30).

Ramesses was desperate to perpetuate his memory, so many of his hieroglyphic inscriptions are cut deep into the stone, some are 15.2cm (6 inches) deep, in an attempt to avoid subsequent kings usurping his monuments because it was cheaper than producing new work. On the Second Pylon the king is depicted with many prisoners; deciphering the hieroglyphics has enabled scholars to identify the third row as being the Philistines, the forbears of Goliath (1 Samuel 17). The Royal Palace is located at the front to the left of the first court. During invasions in the 20th dynasty the entire population of Thebes took refuge within the massive temple walls.

Deir El-Bahri

Hatshepsut was a remarkable woman (see also page 54), and her mortuary temple is one of the most beautiful buildings in Egypt, set against the spectacular backdrop of red cliffs. Senenmut, Hatshepsut's architect (and probably her lover), designed this great structure that rises from the desert in a series of terraces. Ramesses II and his successors later damaged this temple, and later still Christians turned it into a monastery calling it Deir El-Bahri (Northern Monastery).

There are ancient pathways that can still be walked that go to the Valley of the Kings and to the Workmen's Village. Tragically, in 1999 extremists murdered a number of tourists here. Adjacent to Hatshepsut's temple are the remains of the temples of Montuhoptep II and Tuthmosis III and the location of a cache of

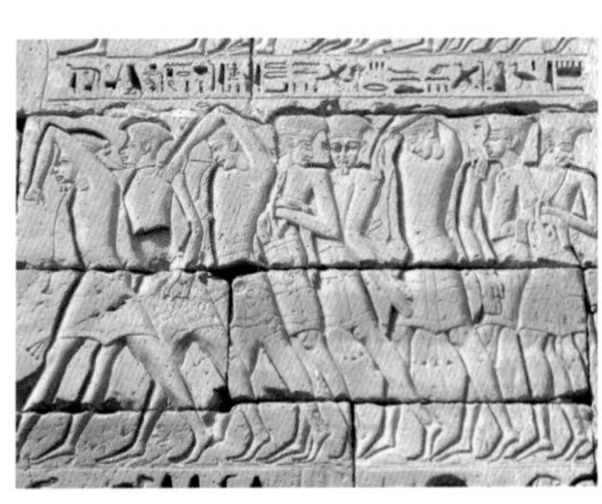

Above: Hatshepsut's beautiful Mortuary temple at Deir El-Bahri

royal mummies where many of the greatest kings were reburied for protection in antiquity.

Deir El-Medina

This is the Workmen's Village where those who constructed the magnificent royal tombs lived. Some of the ancient plaster can still be seen attached to the walls. The whole life of the village was recorded, on one occasion the men complained: 'We are weak and starving because we have not been given the rations which the King ordained', so they stopped working—the first recorded strike in history. The excuses for non-attendance offered by the workers included: one who had to take a sick donkey to the vet, and another who was to bury the same aunt for the third time! An ancient path can still be followed that leads to the Valleys of the Kings and Queens.

Lord Carnarvon

Born in1866, George Edward Stanhope Molyneux Herbert Carnarvon, he sponsored Howard Carter's digs from 1906 to 1922. The 5th Earl of Carnarvon's fascination with Egypt followed a series of motor accidents, as a result of which he was advised to spend winters in a warm climate due to damage to his lungs. He went to the Winter Palace in Luxor and found a new fascination in the relics of the past. His initial excavations were in the region of Thebes. At first he worked alone, but was advised to employ Howard Carter, who had resigned as Chief Inspector of the Egyptian Antiquities Service in 1905. Carter's successful excavations with Lord Carnarvon in the Valley of the Kings in Luxor, include the tombs of Amenhotep I, Hatshepsut, and Thutmose IV. Their greatest achievement was the discovery in 1922 of the tomb of Tutankhamun. Lord Carnarvon died in 1923 before it was thoroughly explored.

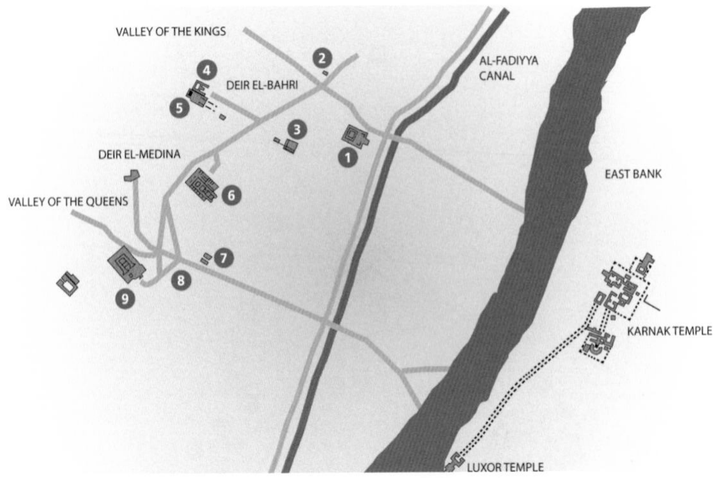

THE WEST BANK LOCATIONS OF FAMOUS SITES

1 TEMPLE OF SETI I
2 HOWARD CARTER'S HOUSE
3 TEMPLE OF RAMESSES IV
4 TEMPLE OF HATSHEPSUT
5 TEMPLE OF MENTUHOTEP
6 RAMESSEUM (TEMPLE OF RAMESSES II)
7 COLOSSI OF MEMNON
8 TICKET OFFICE
9 MEDINET HABU (TEMPLE OF RAMESSES III)

TRAVEL INFORMATION

West Bank

Visiting the West Bank can be by road over the new bridge or by taking a boat over and by hiring a taxi or donkey. Tickets for the various Temples and tombs can be purchased in advance or on the day. Tutankhamun's tomb is so popular that a restriction is now placed on the number of daily visitors permitted. To save disappointment it is best to check in advance whether the tomb will be open when you expect to be there and if it is possible to pre-book tickets. Conservation and preservation of the Temples and Tombs will mean that they are closed on certain days; again, it is wise to check beforehand if you wish to visit a specific site.

Please note that under no circumstances must the paintings in the tombs be touched or defaced. The artwork is ancient and irreplaceable, and any caught doing so are liable to be arrested.

Hot air Balloon flights

These early morning flights are a fabulous way to see the monuments of the west bank, especially the great Temples of the Ramesseum and Medinet Habu. It is best to book these when in Egypt; all the hotels will have details. For the latest archaeological information go to The Theban Mapping project on: www.thebanmappingproject.com

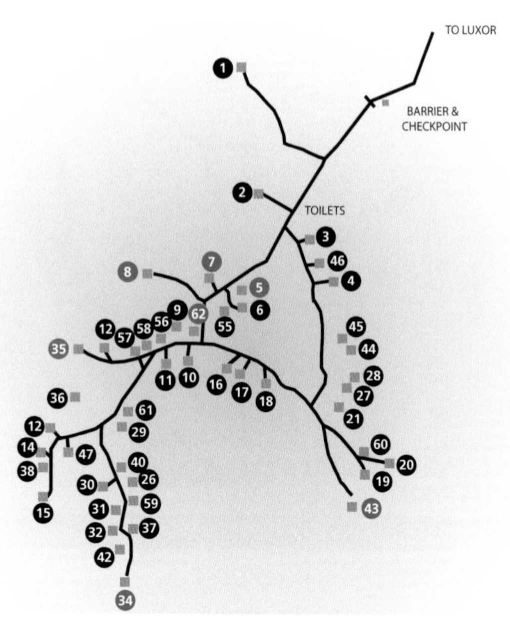

THE VALLEY OF THE KINGS

TOMBS OF INTEREST
5 THE SONS OF RAMESSES II
7 RAMESSES II
8 MERNEPTAH
34 TUTHMOSIS III
35 AMENHOTEP I
43 TUTHMOSIS IV
62 TUTANKHAMUN

Highclere Castle

Highclere Castle
Hampshire, RG20 9RN
www.highclerecastle.co.uk

Sir Charles Barry, who designed the Houses of Parliament created Highclere Castle, the home of Lord Carnarvon. The Castle dominates the magnificent grounds and is the largest mansion in Hampshire, and lies in a beautiful park, the work of Capability Brown during 1774–7. Housed in part of the old cellars is an exhibition of ancient Egyptian finds accumulated from excavations in Thebes and Balamun. Open to the public at selected times during the year. Refreshments and other facilities are available.

Lord Carnarvon's grave is located within an ancient hill fort overlooking his family seat at Beacon Hill, Burghclere, Hampshire 5km (3.1mi) to the south.

***Left:** Highclere Castle's imposing front. This was the home of Lord Carnarvon from 1866 to 1923*

There are no facilities here and the climb to the grave is steep on ground that will be treacherous in inclement weather.

***Right:** The inscription on Lord Carnarvon's grave at Beacon Hill is in poor state*

Putney Vale Cemetery

Stag Lane, Putney
London, SW15 3DZ

Howard Carter's modest grave is number 45, in block 12. The cemetery contains the graves of some of Britain's most celebrated actors, singers, musicians, sportsmen and politicians, including Lady Churchill, wife of Sir Winston, Enid Blyton author, Arthur Askey, Hattie Jacques, Tony Hancock, Kenneth Moore comedians and actors; Roy Plomley presenter, and James Hunt racing driver. Booby Moore captain of the 1966 World Cup winning team was cremated here. The cemetery office has location plans, which can be obtained free.

Swaffham Museum

4 London Street
Swaffham
Norfolk, PE37 7DQ
☎ 🖷 01760 721 230
www.swaffhammuseum.co.uk

Swaffham Museum is situated in the centre of the historic market town of Swaffham in a Grade II listed building built around 1775/1790 on the site of the Great Fire of Swaffham which took place in 1775. A display is dedicated to Howard Carter, who lived in Swaffham, and his famous discovery of the tomb of Tutankhamun.

The Fitzwilliam Museum

Trumpington Street,
Cambridge , CB2 1RB
☎ 01223 332900
🖷 01223 332923
www.fitzmuseum.cam.ac.uk

One of its most important pieces is the famous sarcophagus lid of Ramesses III, given as a gift by Belzoni in 1823.

Sir John Soane's Museum

13 Lincoln's Inn Fields
London, WC2A 3BP
www.soane.org

This houses the huge alabaster sarcophagus of Seti I that was carved in one piece and is intricately decorated on every surface.

***Below:** Howard Carter's modest Grave in Putney Vale Cemetery*

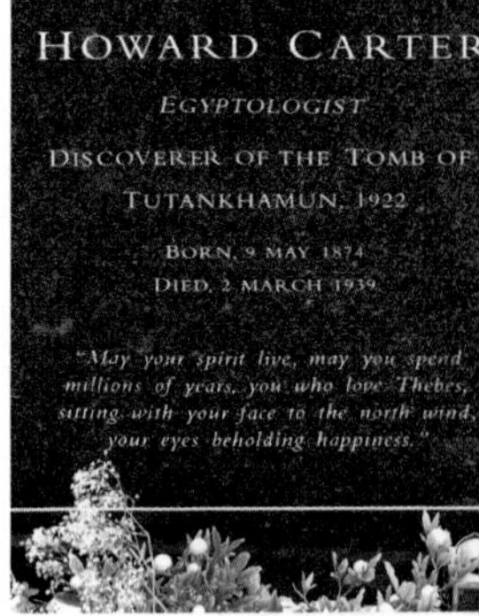

***Above:** The front of Swaffham Museum Norfolk*

8 Along the blue thread

'I have set my first footfall in the East, and Oh! that I could tell you the new world of old poetry, of Bible images, of light, and life, and the beauty which that word opens. My first day in the East, and it has been one of the most striking, I am sure, one I can never forget through eternity'—
Florence Nightingale

Unlike Florence Nightingale in 1849, it is now so much easier to travel through Egypt to experience its delights. Travelling south from Luxor, many places can be visited using a tourist boat on the river, but a few highlights have been selected.

Esna

In ancient times this was one of the most important places in Upper Egypt. Its Egyptian name was *Tesnet,* the Greeks called it *Latopolis* after the Nile perch, because that fish was regarded as sacred and was buried in extensive cemeteries. Esna is one of the main centres of the Coptic faith in Egypt. The remains of the fine Temple of Khnum, which lays 9m (30feet) below the present road level, are an excellent example of how cities and towns grow upward over the centuries with each new generation building upon the ruins of the previous one.

Esna was founded in the Ptolemaic period (332 to 30 BC) and subsequent Roman emperors embellished it with reliefs and inscriptions. The outer walls of the temple bear reliefs and inscriptions of Roman emperors. The south wall shows Domitian smiting his enemy; this emperor may have exiled John to Patmos (Revelation 1:9). The temple façade is 37m (121ft) long and 15m (49ft) high. On the cornice are the names of the Roman emperors Claudius and Vespasian on either side of a winged sun. During the reign of Claudius there was famine (Acts 11:28) and he persecuted the Jews (Acts 18:2). Vespasian started the

Facing page: *A beautiful Ptolemaic composite plant column capital at Philae Temple, showing papyrus sedge and lily plants*

Above: *Boats of all sizes use Esna Lock*

Left: Esna Temple now lies deep below the modern road level

siege of Jerusalem which led to its destruction by his son Titus in AD 70 as predicted by Jesus (Luke 19:43–44, and 21:5–6). On the stone screens between the front columns are depictions of the

Above: *The great Pylon at Edfu Temple with two statues of Horus either side of the entrance*

Pharaoh being led into the temple by various deities.

The Vestibule of the temple, which has seven aisles, is 33m (108ft) long and 16.5m (54ft) wide, and its roof, supported by twenty-four columns, is covered in reliefs and inscriptions that are 11.3m (37ft) high.

Edfu

Edfu was called *Tbot* by the ancient Egyptians, and *Apollinoplis Magna* by the Greeks after the sun god Horus-Apollo who was revered here because, according to legend, it was here that the god Horus fought with the god Seth. The 2,000-year-old temple of Horus is almost perfectly preserved and is the most complete temple complex to visit in Egypt. It looks now almost as it did when the Ptolemys built it, and it gives an idea of the magnificence of Egyptian buildings when Mary and Joseph fled to Egypt with the infant Jesus (Matthew 2:14–15) and during the early church period (Acts 2:10). It was constructed on the site of an earlier temple; the present one was begun in 237 BC by Ptolemy II and completed in 212 BC by Philopater. The inscriptions, which various kings added to, were not completed until 147 BC.

The complex includes a great Pylon with recesses for flag staffs, a 32 columned forecourt adorned with rich flower and palm capitals; then comes the entrance to the vestibule with two colossal Horus falcons wearing the double crown of Upper and Lower Egypt.

The vestibule has 12 columns and a ceiling that is covered with astronomical representations. Beyond, lies the Hypostyle Hall whose roof is also supported by 12 columns, and beyond this are the First and Second antechambers that led into the inner sanctuary. Here, in the sanctuary lit by three small square apertures in the roof, the sacred barque of the god would have been located on the base of black granite.

Moving outside, it is worth walking along the western inner passage where the king is shown trying to spear a hippopotamus; the god Horus is shown in the same posture. The reliefs develop the hunt until the animal is speared in the head. A subterranean staircase leads from the eastern inner passage to an ancient Nilometer; this structure is no longer connected with the River Nile. To the west of the entrance to the temple is the *Mammisi* (birth house), surrounded by columns with figures of the god Bes, who assisted women in labour and childbirth. It may have been a structure similar to this that is referred to when the Pharaoh (Ahmose?) encouraged the Egyptian midwives Shiphrah and Puah, who were probably in charge of many midwives, to kill any Hebrew boys at birth; they refused and gave an interesting reason for disobeying his order—Exodus 1:15–19. High mounds of rubble to the west of the Temple mark the site of the ancient city. Papyri were found here, together with a variety of domestic equipment.

Above: *In Ancient Egypt, Horus was the god synonymous with the power of kingship*

Right: *A Caleche awaits tourists to return them to the boat after a visit to the temple at Edfu*

Kom Ombo and Egyptian medicine

This temple is strategically located on the bend of the Nile near the ancient Egyptian town of Ombos, a place that commanded the trade route from the Nile Valley down into Nubia. The remains of the town lie buried in the sand in the northeast corner of the plateau. This temple is dedicated to two gods: on the left, to Horus the Elder, and on the right, to Sobek the crocodile god, in whose memory a few mummified crocodiles lie to the south of the temple. Adding to the splendour of these buildings, reliefs from Caesar Tiberius (Luke 3:1) are remarkable for their colour and freshness.

Above: The delightful location of Kom Ombo Temple is worth visiting during the day or at night

On the inner wall of the outer corridor, medical instruments including bone-saws, scalpels, birthing stools (Exodus 1:16), suction cups, and dentist tools are illustrated. Egyptian doctors had a widespread reputation for excellence, although they were limited in what they could do for those in need, be it king or commoner. Many ailments are attested: the mummified remains of the Pharaoh Siptah had a severe deformity of the left foot, possibly caused by polio. The gods would be invoked before any consultation, diagnosis or procedure, because religion and medicine were closely linked. Patients would hear one of three statements before a diagnosis: 'This is an ailment I can treat' or, 'This is an ailment I will try to treat' or 'This is an ailment not to be treated'. The Egyptian doctors were familiar with internal organs due to the mummification process, and they knew that the heart was a pump and would say of the pulse: 'It speaks the message of the heart.' A famous papyrus, known as the Edwin Smith papyrus, lists 48 case studies, and it was used to check a range of complaints from fractures to open wounds.

Before a surgical procedure, instruments were sterilized in flame and patients and their surroundings were normally kept clean. Anaesthetics were administered as they did not want the patient to flinch or move; one anaesthetic was made from poppies and this was also used as a painkiller. Open wounds would be stitched, fractures were healed with splints and casts, and there is some evidence that prosthetics were also used.

The Israelites must have been fearful travelling through the wilderness, and in entering the Promised Land, but in Exodus 23:25–26 they were given a conditional promise regarding their health.

Above: *Medical instruments carved on the wall at Kom Ombo are a reminder of the skill of the ancient Egyptian physicians*

Below: *The botanical gardens on Kitchener's Island make a delightful detour for the tourist*

Aswan

Aswan is the jewel of the South, and Egypt's southernmost city. From Old Kingdom times date it guarded Egypt's southern frontier and enabled her forces to make incursions into Nubia and the Sudan. Because Aswan is located on the ancient trade routes between Egypt, Africa and India, it was a great location for the spread of Christianity in the early church. This was the last region to accept Christianity, and it became a sanctuary for Coptic Christians fleeing the advance of Islam; there is still a strong Christian presence here today.

Elephantine

Elephantine is an island in the centre of the River Nile opposite Aswan, and this island was the chief cult centre of Khnum, the ram-headed god. The Elephantine version of the creation myth is recorded on the walls at Esna (see Esna Temple page 101). Khnum is said to have created the universe by modelling the other gods, human beings, animals, birds, fish, reptiles and plants on his potter's wheel (see Nehemiah 9:6 and Romans 9:20–21). On the southern end of the island is an ancient Nilometer, where the steep steps descend into the river. The walls were calibrated to enable the flow of the Nile to be recorded so that Pharaoh's officials could warn

Right: *A juvenile Little Egret, on the side rail of a tourist boat at Aswan, reveals something of the rich variety of bird life in Egypt*

the people if a poor harvest would result from too little or too much water.

The Aswan museum on the centre of the island is home to many artefacts discovered in and around this area.

Kitchener's island

To the west of Elephantine is this delightful place known as the Island of Plants. It was given to the British General Horatio Kitchener as a reward for leading the Egyptian army so successfully in Sudan during the 1890s. He made it his home and filled it with exotic plants and different trees. At dusk the island bird population regales all with their song. Its lush botanical gardens make it a lovely place to stroll or to relax under the trees.

Tombs of the Nobles

North of Kitchener's Island on the west bank of the Nile are the rock-hewn Tombs of the Nobles, some of which are dated to the 6th dynasty (see page 114). At night spotlights illuminate this area.

Aswan high dams

Control of water is a paramount need in guaranteeing a regular crop, and as the population began to rise sharply at the end of the nineteenth century the government decided to take control of the waters of the Nile. The first Dam was completed in 1902, but proved to be inadequate, so additions were made in 1912 and 1934. The dam provides the majority of Egypt's electricity, and a large concrete memorial was set up to celebrate completion of the High Dam in 1971.

The unfinished Obelisk

This is a truly impressive object which, up to a few years ago, could have been walked on; thankfully a fence now protects it. The obelisk is huge and, had it been completed, would have weighed 1,168 tonnes, and stood over 41m (134.5ft) high, but it was abandoned when a major flaw was discovered in the granite. It was planned to be one of a pair with the Lateran Obelisk that is now located in Rome.

Below and right: *The top of Aswan Dam's large concrete memorial can best be photographed by lying on the ground!*

Abu Simbel

The massive temple of Ramesses II is cut into the rock face and extends deep into the rock. This was built to impress and intimidate nations and travellers from the South with the power and might of Egypt and her king. By the time this temple was being constructed, he had

Philae

This wonderful location shows off the superb temple to its best. From here, Isis was said to watch over the sacred island of Biga, one of the mythical burial sites of her husband Osiris (see Abydos page 69). The temples and kiosks are well worth exploring as Egyptian and Roman reliefs are intermingled. The Christian symbols on the temple reveals its change of use, and many Egyptian images have been chiselled out by early Christians to obey the commandment of God in Exodus 20:4 At the northern end of the island, the Temple of Caesar Augustus now lies ruined. Between 1972 and 1980 this temple complex was moved to a new location due to the effects of building the Aswan High Dam.

Above: *The unfinished Obelisk lies in an ancient stone quarry at Aswan*

Above: *The Philae Temple, dedicated to Isis, later became a Christian Church*

Giovanni Belzoni

Giovanni Battista Belzoni was an Italian engineer, barber, monk, and actor, a strongman in a circus—and a giant in nineteenth century Egyptology who has been maligned as a tomb robber. He is perhaps one of the most important and yet least remembered explorers and archaeologists of the past two hundred years. He was born in Padua in 1778 where he first pursued a career as 'The Great Belzoni' a circus strongman before travelling to Egypt in 1814, where he procured large quantities of Egyptian antiquities for European collectors and museums. In 1816 he began to work for Henry Salt, the British Consul-General in Egypt, by helping him to transport the 'young Memnon' the colossal head of Rameses II to England, where it became one of the first Egyptian pieces in the British Museum collection. Belzoni was also the first European to visit the Oasis of Siwa and to penetrate the heart of Khafre's pyramid on the Giza Plateau. Among his many discoveries were six royal tombs in the Valley of the Kings, including that of Seti I, and he excavated the great temple of Abu Simbel after shifting many tons of sand. Belzoni died of dysentery at Benin in December 1823 while trying to reach the source of the River Niger. It has been written about him: 'If you wish to find inspiration for Allen Quatermain and Indiana Jones look no further, for here is a fascinating character.'

Above: *Giovanni Battista Belzoni by William Brockedon*

Right: *Abu Simbel is a mighty reminder of the power of Ramesses II but also of the sublime skill of the Egyptians to produce amazing engineering and artistic work*

assumed divine titles and was known as Ramesses the god. One example of this is recorded when his ministers received reports that the eastern deserts were rich in gold but a shortage of water was making it almost impossible for the workers to survive, they came and prayed to 'Ramesses the god':

> 'You are like Ra in all that you have done, whatever your heart desires comes to pass. If you desire something overnight, comes the dawn and it happens immediately. We have seen so many of your wonderful deeds since you became king of Both Lands. If you say to the water "Come from the mountain", then the water flood shall come forth promptly after your word, because you are Ra in person, the dawning sun in his true form.'

This provides an interesting parallel with the accounts in Exodus 17:3–6 and Numbers 20:2–11.

The planning and construction of this magnificent set of buildings would not have been perceived as problematic. Old and Middle Kingdom (see page 114) graffiti shows that the site Ramesses chose was already considered to be a sacred one. The 33m (110ft) high façade is guarded by four towering colossal statues of Ramesses II, inside are chambers filled with carved columns and walls covered in rich reliefs. On the right hand wall the defeat of the Hittites c1274 BC at Kadesh in Syria is depicted. The temple at Abu Simbel is dedicated to Amun of Thebes, Re-Harakhty of Heliopolis, Ptah of Memphis, and Ramesses himself, of course. This temple was deliberately aligned to allow the sun at dawn on 20 February and 20 October to shine

Left: *Two of the great heads of Ramesses II at Abu Simbel*

into the innermost sanctuary and for five minutes to illuminate the statues of these four gods.

Ramesses' beloved Queen Nefertari is honoured by the smaller temple, which is dedicated to Hathor. His love for her is revealed in that her statues are the same size as his and the goddesses. The inside decoration reveals Ramesses and Nefertari making offerings to the gods, and scenes of the king slaying Egypt's enemies under the admiring gaze of his wife.

During the 1960s UNESCO moved these temples to an artificially constructed cliff to save them from the rising water of Lake Nasser.

***Above:** Relaxing in a Jacuzzi after a hard day sightseeing is something to look forward too*

Lake Nasser

At 500km (310mi) long and over 180m (590ft) deep in places, this is the largest artificial lake in the world. It was created by the construction of the Aswan High Dam and flooded a huge expanse of land from Aswan to Abu Simbel to ensure a regular water supply into Egypt.

To Nubia

Nubia, (southern Sudan) to the South was a rich source of minerals and gold for the ancient Egyptians. To ensure a regular supply, fortresses were constructed to protect the trade routes. During the New Kingdom, Egypt ruled Nubia directly, and several temples were constructed to help maintain tight control over the territory. Sailing on Lake Nasser and visiting some of the temples is an enriching experience.

The end—not yet

Egypt not only has a long and fascinating history, but continual discoveries reveal a rich past that helps to enliven the present with promises of continual pleasures for the traveller to the 'blessed land.'

TRAVEL INFORMATION

Abu Simbel

Although it can be reached by road it is easiest to travel by air. The great Temple complex lays 280km (175mi) south of Aswan and 40km (25mi) north of the Egyptian/Sudanese frontier at Wadi Halfa.

Aswan

Lies 950km (590mi) south of Cairo and can be reached by road, rail, air or by cruise ship along the Nile.

Because of its climate Aswan is noted for its cleanliness and the friendly nature of the inhabitants and is a favoured winter resort.

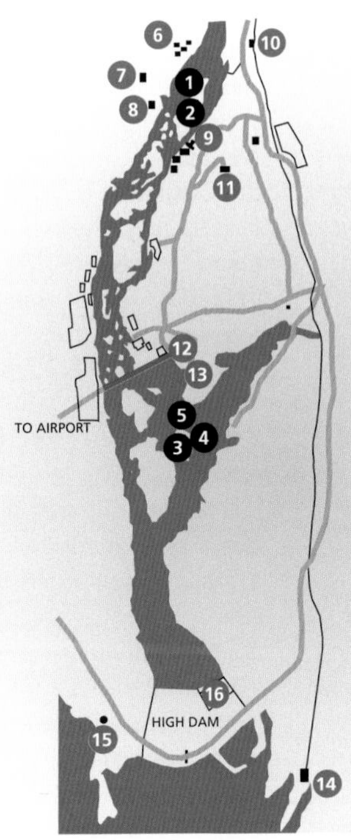

ISLANDS

1 KITCHENER'S
2 ELEPHANTINE
3 BIGA
4 PHILAE (MOSTLY SUBMERGED)
5 AGLIKA (TEMPLE OF PHILAE)
6 ROCK TOMBS
7 ST. SIMEON'S MONASTARY
8 MAUSOLEUM OF THE AGA KHAN
9 OLD CATARACT HOTEL
10 STATION
11 UNFINISHED OBELISK
12 ASWAN DAM
13 BOATS FOR AGLIKA
14 TERMINUS NILE VALLEY RAILWAY
15 MONUMENT
16 HYDRO ELECTRIC STATION

THE AREA AROUND ASWAN

Aswan High Dam

A visit to the top of the Dam gives an impressive view of this engineering feat. Information boards show how the Dam works.

Old Cataract Hotel

Abtal El Tahrir Street
Aswan,
☎ 00 20 97 231 6000
www.sofitel.com

The Old Cataract Hotel is a splendidly atmospheric place, which has always attracted a mix of famous figures: Winston Churchill, Agha Khan, King Farouk, Princes Diana and Agatha Christie, who wrote Death on the Nile here. Perched on a rock facing the southern tip of Elephantine Island, it is worth slipping into the terrace bar for a refreshing drink and panoramic views of the Nile.

Kom Ombo

This Temple is situated 40km (25mi) north of Aswan and can be reached by road or rail, but is best seen from the River Nile. There is a fine market on the quayside that sells clothing and many souvenirs. Also, snake charmers ply their trade close by.

Philae

It is 6 km (4mi) South from Aswan to the landing stage. Boats can be hired by a group or individually to the Temple site on the island. An impressive sound and light show is held here each night in different languages, timings for each showing can be ascertained in Aswan.

Glossary of terms

Note that not all the terms listed here are found in this Travel Guide, but they may be used by tour guides in Egypt.

Amulet A charm usually worn or carried.

Ankh Egyptian word for life carried by gods and offered to kings.

Ba Personality portrayed as a human-headed bird.

Barque A boat-shaped shrine.

Cartouche A cartridge shaped enclosure (from the French *cartouche*) with a horizontal line at one end, indicating that the text enclosed is a royal name. As time went on, many people hired an artist to create a cartouche for their own coffins.

Cuneiform The wedge-shaped signs of Babylonian and Assyrian writing used from about 2,000 BC.

Cursive Letters of the alphabet that were joined together in writing. In Greek this joining took place around the 7th century AD.

Demotic script The cursive form of Egyptian hieroglyphics used for ordinary documents in Egypt from around 650BC to AD 500. The word means 'of the people' and refers to writing that was in a popular, commonly used form by ordinary people.

Dyad A pair of statues often carved from the same block.

Dynasty A line of rulers generally from the same family (see page 114).

Execration texts Curses upon foreign rulers and places used to destroy magically Egypt's enemies.

Fertile Crescent The territory stretching from Egypt in the south through Palestine, Syria and Mesopotamia in the north and then down to the Persian Gulf. It forms a large crescent shape of the most fertile land.

Heb sed Royal jubilee festival celebrated by the king after thirty years rule.

Hieratic script A shortened form of Egyptian hieroglyphs for writing on papyrus.

Hieroglyphic The earliest writing from Egypt and elsewhere that represents a word, syllable or sound in the form of pictures. From the Greek meaning 'a sacred carving'.

Hypostyle Hall Columned and roofed temple court.

Ka Vital force/sustenance, pictorially represented as a person's double.

Lapis lazuli The mineral sodium aluminium silicate and sulphur in the form of a bright blue gemstone that was commonly used for jewellery. It was mined in Afghanistan.

Levant The lands to the east of the Mediterranean where the sun rises; from French *lever*—to rise.

Mastaba A tomb with a mound shaped superstructure over a subterranean burial chamber.

Minuscule (var. miniscule) Lower case letters that were later joined up into cursive writing in the 7th century AD. The opposite of uncial.

Mummy From Arabic mummia meaning bitumen or rock-like as mummies ended up being black and hard. They were not, as once thought, mummified by using bitumen.

Nemes The most common royal headdress, thought possibly to made from cloth to mimic the hood of the cobra, with the Uraeus on the brow.

Nilometer The measuring gauge used to record the flood levels of the Nile. Originally a marble well decorated with two copper eagles, male and female.

Nomes The provinces of ancient Egypt, of which there were 20 in Lower and 22 in Upper Egypt.

Obelisk A four-sided, stone pillar tapering at the top; usually inscribed with texts as a monument or record.

Pharaoh The title of the kings of Egypt from around 14th century BC. The word comes from the Egyptian 'per-aa' meaning 'a great house'.

Peristyle Court Open colonnade temple court.

Porphyry A hard rock, largely composed of crystals, quarried in ancient Egypt.

Potsherd A piece of broken pottery or glass, see also Shard, frequently used for scribbled notes when it is known as 'ostrachon'.

Pyramids Gigantic tombs. The shape represents a theory of creation.

Pylon The gateway into a temple area.

Relief Raised relief in which the objects stand out from the background.

Sunken relief in which the objects are let into the background.

Sarcophagus A stone coffin often sculptured or inscribed. It comes from a Greek word meaning 'flesh-eating'.

Scarab Dung beetle amulet of creation, rebirth and new life.

Shabti Funerary figurine placed in a burial to act as the deputy for the deceased when called upon to perform menial tasks in the afterlife.

Shard See Potsherd. A variant of 'sherd' a short form of potsherd.

Stela An upright pillar with an inscription and sometimes a sculpture.

Syncretism The fusion of two gods into one; for example Amun-Ra.

Uncial The early form of modern capital letters; the uncials, which are un-joined letters, are found in Greek manuscripts from the 4th to 8th centuries AD.

***Right:** Papyrus and Lotus on columns at Karnak temple*

Ancient Egyptian timeline

Manetho, a priest who wrote a history of Ancient Egypt in the third century BC, divided it into dynasties for convenience.

Period	Date	Dynasties
Predynastic	before 3120BC	
Archaic	3120–2686BC	1 and 2
Old Kingdom	2686–2181BC	3 to 6
1st Intermediate Period	2181–2040BC	7 to 10
Middle Kingdom	2040–1786BC	11 and 12
2nd Intermediate Period	1786–1567BC	13 to 17
New Kingdom	1567–1085BC	18 to 20
3rd Intermediate Period	1085–664BC	21 to 25
Late Period	664–332BC	26 to 30
Ptolemaic	332–30BC	31

In 30BC the Romans invaded Egypt and it became a province of the Roman Empire, ceasing to be an independent nation.

Above: *Wall decoration at the Ramesses II temple at Abydos*

Chronology of the major pyramids

Pharaoh	Reign BC approximate dates	Location
Zoser	2630–2612	Saqqara
Sneferu (bent)	2612–589	Dashur
Sneferu (red)	2612–2589	Dashur
Sneferu (ruined)	2612–2589	Meidum
Khufu (Cheops)	2589–2566	Giza
Djedefre	2566–2558	Abu Rawash
Khafre (Chephren)	2558–2532	Giza
Menkaure (Mykerinus)	2532–2504	Giza
Sahure	2487–2477	Abu Sir
Neferirkare Kakai	2477–2467	Abu Sir
Nyuserre Ini	2416–2392	Abu Sir
Amenemhat I	1991–1962	Lisht
Senusret I	1971–1926	Lisht
Senusret II	1897–1878	el-Lahun
Amenemhat III	1860–1814	Hawara

Above: *Ancient and modern*

List of Egyptian kings with Bible connections

A precise chronology for the dynasties of Egypt is not possible. We have listed only those Pharaohs associated with the Bible.

King	BC	Bible
Khety II	2115–2070	Abraham into Egypt about 2091BC (Genesis 12:10–20).
Amenemhat II	1922–1878	Joseph probably entered his service in 1885 (Genesis 41:41).
Sesostris II	1880–1874	Jacob settled in Egypt (Genesis 47:9)
Sesostris III	1874–1855	Joseph probably Prime Minister (Vizier) in his reign and Jacob died.
Amenemhet IV	1808–1799	Joseph died during his reign in 1806.
Ahmose	1550–1526	Ordered the death of the Hebrew boys (Exodus 1:15–16).
Amenhotep I	1526–1504	Or this was the Pharaoh responsible for the above.
Tuthmosis II	1492–1479	Moses fled from Egypt (Exodus 2:15).
Tuthmosis III	1479–1425	The Pharaoh of the oppression and/or the Exodus if we take an early date for the Exodus.
Amenhotep II	1427–1400	Or the Pharaoh of the Exodus if we take an early date for the Exodus. Part co-regency with Tuthmosis III. Joshua enters the Promised Land of Canaan.
Tuthmosis IV	1400–1390	Joshua conquers the Promised Land.
Amenhotep III	1390–1352	See the Amarna Letters (page 67).

Left: *The back of Tutankhamun's funerary mask containing spell 151b of the book of the dead*

Amenhotep IV (Akhenaten)	1352–1336	The 'heretic pharaoh' (page 67).
Tutankhamun	1336–1327	Items from his tomb illustrate many biblical objects.
Ramesses II	1279–1213	The Pharaoh of the Exodus if we take a late date for the Exodus.
Merneptah	1213–1203	First recorded mention of Israel (page 50).
Siamun	978–959	Possibly the Pharaoh when Solomon sealed an alliance by marrying his daughter (1 Kings 3:1).
Shoshenq I*	945–924	The biblical Shishak who sacked the temple in Jerusalem in 925 (1 Kings 14:25).
Osorkon IV*	734–715	The grandson of Shishak, referred to in 2 Kings 17:4 as So.
Taharqa*	690–664	Tirhakah who threatened Sennacherib (2 Kings 19:9).
Tantamani	664–656	Assyrian king Ashurbanipal sacked Thebes (Nahum 3:8–10).
Necho II*	610–595	Defeated Josiah and imprisoned Jehoahaz (2 Kings 23:29 to 35).
Apries*	589–570	The Hophra referred to in Jeremiah 44:30.
Augustus*	27BC to AD14	Augustus was the first Roman Emperor to take the title of Pharaoh in Egypt. Joseph took Mary and the infant Christ to Egypt (Matthew 2:13).
Arab conquest	AD 640	Muslim invaders reduced the Christian church.

* These kings are mentioned by name in the Bible

Right: *A diorite statue of Pharaoh Khafre, builder of the 2nd pyramid at Giza which Abraham would have seen*

Chief gods of Egypt

Egyptian religion was complex, with over 1500 gods who were worshipped in specific ways in local temples by specialised priesthoods or locally in communities. To modern eyes the overlapping of myths and legends seems curiously contradictory, but the Egyptians did not demand consistency of their theology. So do not be surprised if you are confused by their beliefs!

Amun/Amun-Re King of the gods, Husband of Mut and the father of Khonsu.

Anubis Canine god of embalming and cemeteries.

Aten Solar disk, (Sun) under Akhenaten (1379–1362BC) became the almost exclusive deity (page 65).

Atum Sun-god and creator of the universe. The setting Sun, father of the Ennead. Frequently called 'Lord of Heliopolis,' (Iunu in Egyptian and On in the Bible). It was the centre for Sun worship.

Bastet Cat-headed woman, daughter of Re.

Ennead Greek word for nine and is the company of nine gods originally at Heliopolis consisting of the sun-god—Atum—and his descendants.

Hapy God of the annual inundation.

Hathor Mother goddess, symbolic mother of the Pharaoh, daughter of Re

Harakhty The morning Sun.

Horus Sky god, symbol of divine kingship, Son of Osiris and Isis.

Eye of Horus Seth had cut out Horus' eyes after a great battle. Hathor restored his eyes, and as a result a single eye became the symbol of protection, many amulets and pictorial representations of this.

Isis Mother goddess, goddess of immense magical power, symbolic mother of the King and mother of Horus.

Khepri The rising Sun and Sun-god creator in the form of a scarab beetle (the dung beetle).

Khonsu (sometimes **Khons**) Moon-god especially prominent at Thebes.

Khnum Creator of life on the potter's wheel and guardian of source of Nile.

Maat Goddess of balance, harmony, truth and justice.

Min God of fertility.

Mut Vulture-headed goddess, wife of Amun.

Neith Warrior goddess.

Nut Sky goddess.

Ogdoad Eight deities representing the primeval chaos before the emergence of the sun-god.

Osiris God of the underworld, husband of Isis and father of Horus.

Pharaoh Literally per-aa, meaning 'great house', he is called 'the beautiful god.' Each king was a combination of the divine and the mortal. The vulture goddesses of the South, Nekhbet, and the royal cobra for the North, Wadjet, are normally shown on the king's everyday headdress symbolising his control of both Upper and Lower Egypt.

Ptah God of creation and craftsman, husband of Sekhmet.

Ra (sometimes **Re**) Creator Sun god, father of Maat, he is the quintessence of all manifestations of the sun-god, permeating the three realms of the sky, earth and underworld. Linked in the new Kingdom to Amun.

Sekhmet Lion-headed goddess of desert, storm and pestilence, daughter of Re and the wife of Ptah.

Seth God of chaotic forces who commands both veneration and hostility.

Sobek God of water and fertility.

Thoth Moon-god and patron of scribes and knowledge.

Wepwawet Jackal-god portrayed on the Narmer tablet, in the Pyramid texts he performed the opening of the mouth ceremony.

Known Tombs in the Valley of the Kings

Tomb numbers are prefaced with KV, which refers to the Kings' Valley

KV 1	Ramesses VII	KV 32	unknown
KV 2	Ramesses IV	KV 33	unknown
KV 3	Ramesses III	KV 34	Tuthmosis III
KV 4	Ramesses XI	KV 35	Amenhotep II
KV 5	Sons of Ramesses II	KV 36	Maiherperi
KV 6	Ramesses IX	KV 37	unknown
KV 7	Ramesses II	KV 38	Tuthmosis I
KV 8	Merneptah	KV 39	unknown
KV 9	Ramesses V / VI	KV 40	unknown
KV 10	Amenmeses	KV 41	unknown
KV 11	Ramesses III	KV 42	Hatshepsut-Meryetre
KV 12	unknown	KV 43	Tuthmosis IV
KV 13	Bay	KV 44	Anen (?)
KV 14	Tausert / Setnakht	KV 45	Userhet
KV 15	Seti II	KV 46	Yuya and Thuya
KV 16	Ramesses I	KV 48	Amenemopet
KV 17	Seti I	KV 49	Maya (?)
KV 18	Ramesses X	KV 50	animals
KV 19	Mentuherkhepshef	KV 51	animals
KV 20	Hatshepsut	KV 52	animals
KV 21	two queens	KV 53	unknown
WV 22	Amenhotep III	KV 54	Tutankhamun
WV 23	Ay	KV 55	Smenkhkara
WV 24	unknown	KV 56	unknown
WV 25	Akhenaten (?)	KV 57	Horemheb
KV 26	unknown	KV 58	Ay
KV 27	unknown	KV 59	unknown
KV 28	unknown	KV 60	two women
KV 29	unknown	KV 61	unknown
KV 30	unknown	KV 62	Tutankhamun
KV 31	unknown		

Left: *Statue of Anubis from the tomb of Tutankhamun*

Information for those travelling in Egypt

Time is GMT +2 hours. Weights and Measures are Metric and the Voltage is 220v AC. Sockets take standard continental 2 pin round plugs.

Medical. Egypt requires some inoculations, so see your GP in good time to arrange for these to be administered. Stomach upsets are blamed on the food, but are more likely to be caused by too much sun, drinking alcohol or not washing hands before eating. Also take anti-bacterial hand wipes and paper tissues.

Pack medicine in case of an upset stomach and modify your diet if you do develop a gastric problem. Hotels and tourist boats can provide plain boiled rice which is excellent for upset stomachs. Also drinking coke is quite good for a stomach upset.

Remember to drink plenty of water, as it is important to urinate at least three times a day. If urine is dark in colour, it is a warning sign of dehydration. In extreme cases this can be dangerous and lead to hospitalisation. See Water and Other drinks.

Insect repellent is a must and aim to keep as much skin covered in the evenings (long sleeved top / long trousers and socks). Take antihistamine cream to deal immediately with any bites so they do not get infected. It is wise to check with your GP about malaria medication.

Documents. Photocopy or scan your passport, travel insurance, repeat prescription form, and glasses specification. Take a copy of these with you and leave a copy together with your itinerary with a contact person at home. It is also wise to scan your credit cards; if they are lost or stolen a rapid stop can be placed on them therefore you will need to have contact details of your credit card company with you.

Luggage and labelling for home details. Label your entire luggage with only your name, tour operator and first hotel. For home use only a house number and post code. Put full details with a list of where you will be staying inside the locked case. Follow carefully the airline instructions for what not to carry in your hand luggage. You will want to carry with you each day; water, hat, sun cream, camera, tissues etc, so pack a bag for this. Ladies are advised to pack a spare bra in your hand luggage, as this item may prove difficult to replace should your main luggage go missing.

Things to wear. Do not expect to walk around in new or tight shoes. It is hot, dry and dusty. Your feet will swell, so wear old and comfortable shoes. Take loose cotton clothing, as this will help you to stay cool and comfortable. Egypt is a Muslim country so please be sensitive to their customs. Dress modestly: ladies, if you can avoid shorts and bare shoulders then do so; though if you wish to wear sleeveless tops and not too short shorts during the daytime it should be OK; on a tour you will be informed when they are not appropriate. Carry a light shawl to cover your arms if requested. Shorts during the daytime are normally acceptable for men, unless you are visiting a designated holy site, like a mosque.

It is best to change for the evening meal. As dining rooms, especially on a boat, are much cooler than the surrounding areas, take a cardigan, light jacket or an extra layer (shirt to go over T-shirt). Also if you are attending the sound and light shows (especially Karnak and Philae) you will be out near water at dusk and in the dark. Note the comment about insect repellent under Medical above.

Hat, Sunscreen and sunglasses. A hat is a must, as is a good sunscreen cream. Do not ruin your holiday with painful (even dangerous) sunburn. You will need to wear sunglasses during the day.

Small Torch. This is useful for looking more closely at items or carvings where the light is not good. It is also useful when you are coming back from a sound and light show as it will be dark and paths are uneven.

Money. The unit of currency is the Egyptian pound (E) in which there are 100 piastres (PT). There are notes for piastres (don't accept coins) and 1, 5, 10, 20 pound notes. Egyptian money is very well handled and clean crisp notes are virtually non-existent. We would advise keeping your Egyptian money in a separate plastic wallet, as it is often dirty and smelly. Take single US dollar bills to use as tips as the smallest English note is 5 whereas $1 is acceptable to the Egyptians. It is easy to check currency rates on the net. There are ATM machines in banks and some hotels, but before you leave, you are advised to inform your card provider that you will be using it abroad.

Water. Tap water in Egypt is very heavily chlorinated and currently it is advised not to drink this or clean your teeth with it. Mineral water is readily available in the hotels and at kiosks. Make sure the seal is intact, as sometimes empty bottles are refilled with tap water. It is cheaper to buy the big bottles of water but these are heavy to carry around; you might like to take a small water bottle with you to decant water into.

Other drinks. For any drinks that are not in a clear bottle it is wisest to tip a little into your hand to check that it is what you expected, as it is not unknown for bottles to be filled with Nile water and the top jammed back on. It is best to avoid alcohol, as it will dehydrate you.

Food. Most of the hotels cater for the western diet, although some food will be flavoured slightly differently.

An Egyptian breakfast usually consists of a combination of the following: egg (boiled, omelette, scrambled), bread (not toast), fruit, yoghurt, pastries, fruit juice, tea or coffee, with milk being dried and reconstituted. It is best to peel fruit or wipe it well before you eat it. It is advisable to bring some biscuits or cereal bars. Although chocolate, crisps and biscuits are available for purchase they are often quite different from the same product at home. If you do get a stomach upset, it is sometimes helpful and comforting to eat something that your body is familiar with.

We would advise against buying food from street vendors. If you choose to do so, and if it is unwrapped, look at the seller's hands, and the standard of hygiene at his stall. Nuts, spices, pre-packed food should be OK. Agree a price (see bargaining) before you pick up something. Because Egypt is hotter than England, you will perspire more. To counteract salt loss, take a little salt with your food even if you do not do this at home.

USEFUL WORDS

La No (very useful if you feel you are being bothered), say 'La' with feeling and raise your hand, but do no touch the other person—that is offensive.

Aywa	Yes.
Shukran	Thank you.
Afwan	You are welcome.
Inshallah	God willing.
Sabaah al-kheir	Good morning
Salaam aleikum	Hello
Feyn el-twalet	Where is the toilet?
Shai	Tea
Ahwa	Coffee

BARGAINING

In a Souk (market), some shop and taxis, bargaining is expected. Most sellers start at a price 2 or 3 times higher than the amount they hope to make. Decide a price you are happy to pay and then start lower. Always be polite and good-humoured and ask before you pick up something. If the final price does not suit then just walk away. Give it a go. If you want more than one of the same item bargain for one and then state how many you want and lower the price per item for the total amount. Please remember that most of the things you buy will be souvenirs / luxuries for you, but for the seller they are part of his limited income.

BAKSHEESH / TIPS

The common workforce is not paid high wages and all rely on 'Baksheesh' or tips to survive. Everyone expects baksheesh for services rendered, not just from tourists, Egyptians are also expected to tip. If all tips for the hotels, guides, drivers etc are included in the cost of your tour you will normally need additionally to tip for the following: Taxi or caleche (horse drawn cart) if you use them. Buying lunch (except on the boat when it is usually provided), 12½% is usually added to bill but an extra tip of about 10% is normal and expected. Toilet attendant (you will not be given toilet paper if you don't give a tip); if you do you will possibly get two squares! It is best to bring plenty of tissues or a roll paper with you. Have small bills ready. (E1 is less than 10p). Tip often (small amounts) as tips might be the person's only income.

***Below:** Esna boat sellers*

A taste of Egypt

Om Ali—a very rich Egyptian type of bread-and-butter pudding.

This is a desert whose name roughly translated means 'Ali's mother's pudding'. It is sweet and very rich and creamy and we have eaten many different variations, some more to our taste than others, but none ever disappointing. We suggest you try it. It is often served as part of the 'Egyptian evening' buffet, but if you are choosing from a menu then ask for it when you order your main course, as it takes a while to cook, but say that it is to be served as the dessert. Here is our delicious version that you can try at home.

***Above:** Omi Ali, a delicious Egyptian pudding*

Ingredients

500g (1lb) puff pastry (shop bought is fine).
1000ml (35 fl oz) milk.
450ml (15 fl oz) double cream.
100g (3oz) pistachio nuts and 50g (2oz) pine kernels (or you can use roughly chopped mixed nuts).
150g (5oz) sultanas.
150g (5oz) white sugar.

Method

Preheat oven to 220°C / 425°F / Gas mark 7.

Roll out the pastry 1cm thick. Cut into pieces (they don't have to be uniform just roughly 5cm / 2inch squares). Place the pieces on a baking sheet and cook for about 10 minutes until puffed. Leave to cool slightly.

Break pastry pieces along the layers until about 1/2 cm. Butter a dish or tin and put alternate layers of pastry, nuts and sultanas in, finishing with a layer of pastry.

Put the milk and sugar into a large saucepan and heat until sugar is dissolved and the milk is just below boiling point. Take off the heat and stir in the cream. Carefully pour most of the milk mixture over the pastry, nuts and sultanas (the pastry will float, so push it down with a spatula and leave for a bit to soak up the milk then add the rest of the milk). Leave for 10 minutes (to let the cream rise to the top) and then put in the oven and bake for 20–30 minutes or until brown and bubbling. Serve hot.

It can be frozen, cooked or uncooked. If it has been cooked then it can successfully be reheated in a microwave.

Index of Egyptian place names

Left: *Howard Carter. Discovered and excavated Tutanhkamun's tomb in the Valley of the Kings in 1922.*

Acknowledgements

Pictures

Clive and Amanda Anderson and friends: Denis Cocks, Tom Ellenden, Stephen Evans, Mark Hamilton, Jocelyn Pimm of Worldwide Christian Travel, Charles and Sandra Lambert, Tim Pinchen, John Sills, Philip West.

Thanks also to those who have added their pictures copyright free to Wikimedia commons: egyptarchive, Hans Hillewaert, Markh, McLeod. Pedro A. Rodriguez, Sebi,

Information

Mrs Valerie Offord for details regarding Charles Bousfield Huleatt

Authors

Clive and Amanda have a long standing interest in ancient Egypt and have visited it many times. They have also travelled the world visiting museums and collections connected with Egyptology. Clive has authored other books for Day One and is a member of the Egypt Exploration Society and the British Institute for the Study of Iraq

Clive and Amanda have one son, Luke, and they live and work in Alton, Hampshire, UK.

Day One Audio books

Some of the Travel Guides are available as audio books to download. Go to www.dayone.co.uk and click on Audio Books. Currently available as an audio book: Travel with William Tyndale, Travel with John Calvin and Travel with Billy Graham.

The Egypt Exploration Society

The EES was founded in 1882, and has from its inception, made surveys, conducted explorations and excavations in Egypt and the Sudan for the purpose of obtaining information about the ancient history, religion, arts, literature, and ethnology of those countries.

Anyone interested in the promotion of the Society's objectives is eligible for election as a member. Depending on the level joined, membership entitles one to the Journal, or the Graeco-Roman Memoirs. All members receive Egyptian Archaeology (twice a year) and can purchase the Society's publications at a discount, as well as read in the Library. For any who have or wish to pursue an interest in Egyptology the EES is a marvellous resource of scholarship and up to date news.

Full particulars may be obtained from the Membership Secretary. Website: www.ees.ac.uk

DAY ONE TRAVEL GUIDES

This series is unique: each book combines biography an history with travel guide. Notes, maps and photographs help you to explore Britain's distinctive heritage.

128 pages **£10 EACH**

- PLACES OF INTEREST
- PACKED WITH COLOUR PHOTOS
- CLEAR ILLUSTRATED MAPS
- GREAT GIFT IDEA

ALSO AVAILABLE

Through the British Mueum:
with the Bible

Discover the many Bible related exhibits at Britain's most popular tourist destination.

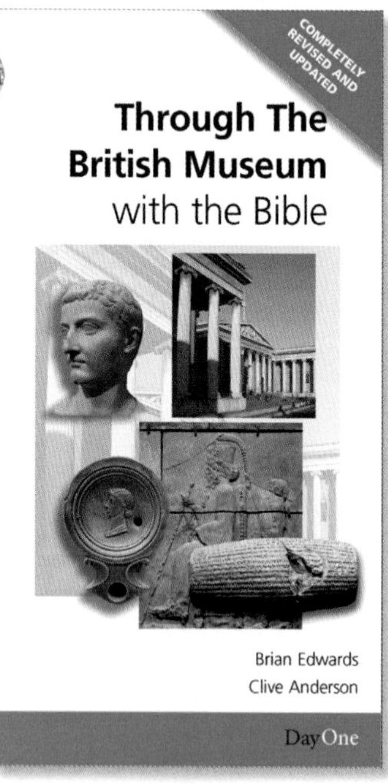

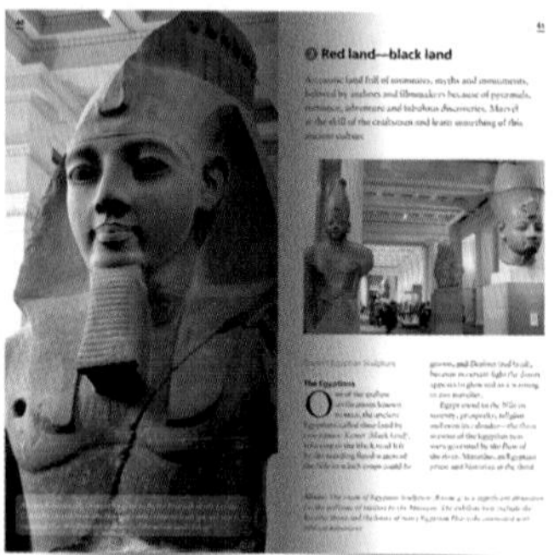

ORDER TODAY

CALL DAYONE PUBLICATIONS ON ✆ 01568 613740 AND ORDER TODAY

FOOTSTEPS OF THE PAST

A series of children's activity books twinned with the Travel Guides

ROMANS, GLADIATORS AND GAMES
In the British Museum, explore the Roman world of the first Christians.

KINGS, PHARAOHS AND BANDITS
In the British Museum, explore the world of Abraham to Esther.

WILLIAM TYNDALE
He was threatened, hunted, betrayed and killed so that we could have the Bible in English

Permission is given to copy the activity pages and associated text for use as class or group material

EGYPT
Ancient Egypt and the Bible

JOHN BUNYAN
How a hooligan and solidier became a preacher, prisoner and famous writer

WILLIAM CAREY
The story of a country boy and shoe mender whose big dreams took him to India

WILLIAM BOOTH
The troublesome teenager who changed the lives of people no one else would touch

WILLIAM WILBERFORCE
The millionaire child who worked so hard to win the freedom of African slaves.

C S LEWIS
The story of one of the world's most famous authors who sold over a hundred million books

OTHER TITLES IN THIS SERIES

Travel with...

JOHN BUNYAN
C H SPURGEON
WILLIAM BOOTH
JOHN KNOX
MARTYN LLOYD-JONES
WILLIAM GRIMSHAW
WILLIAM CAREY
WILLIAM WILBERFORCE
C S LEWIS
ROBERT MURRAY McCHEYNE
MARTYRS OF MARY TUDOR
JOHN CALVIN
WILLIAM TYNDALE
JOHN BLANCHARD
BILLY GRAHAM

Travel through...

THE BRITISH MUSEUM
OXFORD
CAMBRIDGE
ISRAEL

MORE TITLES ARE IN PREPARATION

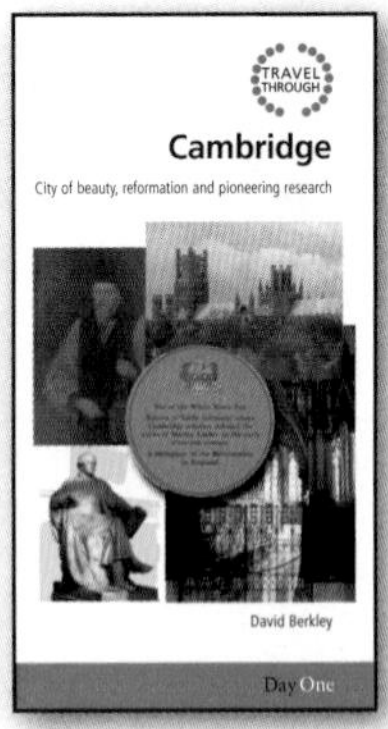